the Forth Naturalist and Historian

Volume 31 2008

Published by the Forth Naturalist and Historian, University of Stirling – charity SCO 13270.

ISSN 0309-7560

ISBN 1-898-008-65-5

Supported by INEOS and Scottish Natural Heritage.

Cover: front– Sir John Murray commemorated on a Christmas Island stamp.
    (Reproduced with permission of the Australian Postal
    Corporation. The original work is held in the National
    Philatelic Collection.)
    back– The Challenger Medal designed by John Murray portraying a
    knight throwing down his gauntlet as a challenge to the ocean
    to give up its secrets. Awarded to all those who contributed to
    the 50 volumes of the Challenger Expedition Report
    (© National Maritime Museum, Greenwich, London).

Printed by Meigle Colour Printers Ltd., Tweedbank Industrial Estate, Galashiels.
Set in Zapf Calligraphic on Amber 100 gsm and cover 300 gsm Satin.

THE FORTH NATURALIST AND HISTORIAN

The Forth Naturalist and Historian (FNH) is an informal enterprise of Stirling University. It was set up in 1975 by several University and Central Regional Council staff to provide a focus for interests, activities and publications of environmental, heritage and historical studies for the Forth area, comprising now local authority areas Stirling, Falkirk and Clackmannanshire.

Since then the organisation of an annual environment/heritage symposium called *Man and the Landscape* has been an important feature.

The annual *Forth Naturalist and Historian* has published numerous papers, many being authoritative and significant in their field, and includes annual reports of the weather, and of birds in the locality, plus book reviews and notes. These volumes provide a valuable successor to that basic resource *The Transactions of the Stirling Field and Archaeological Society, 1878-1939.* Four year contents/indexes are available, and selected papers are published in pamphlet form, while others are available as reprints.

In addition a 230 page book *Central Scotland – Land, Wildlife, People,* a natural history and heritage survey, was produced in 1994 and is available in the form of a CD-Rom, *Heart of Scotland's Environment* (HSE).

Other FNH and associated publications still in print include – *Mines and Minerals of the Ochils, Airthrey and Bridge of Allan, Woollen Mills of the Hillfoots, The Ochil Hills* – landscape, wildlife, heritage – an introduction with walks, *Alloa Tower and the Erskines of Mar,* and the *Lure of Loch Lomond* a journey round the shores and islands. Several of these are in association with Clackmannanshire Field Studies Society.

FNH publications are listed on the internet British Library (BLPC) and by booksellers e.g. Amazon, Bol, Barnes and Noble.

Offers of papers/notes for publication, and of presentations for symposia are ever welcome.

Honorary Secretary Marilyn Scott,
Computer Services, University of Stirling, FK9 4LA.
E-mail: fnh@stir.ac.uk
Web: http://www.fnh.stir.ac.uk

Author Addresses

Tertia Barnett, Royal Commission on the Ancient and Historic Monuments of Scotland, Edinburgh

Neil Bielby, 56 Ochiltree, Dunblane FK15 0DF

David Bytheway, 5 The Meadows, Coalsnaughton FK13 6LW

Alastair Durie, History, The University, Stirling

Angela Gannon, Royal Commission on the Ancient and Historic Monuments of Scotland, Edinburgh

Karl Magee, The Library, The University, Stirling

Ron Page, Kingarth, Airthrey Road, Stirling FK9 5PH

Roy Sexton, 22 Alexander Drive, Bridge of Allan FK9 4QB

Malcolm Shaw, 5 Pendreich Road, Bridge of Allan FK9 4LY

REBIRTH OF A RAILWAY

David Bytheway

The opening of the Stirling-Alloa-Kincardine railway in May, 2008 was a red letter day for the Wee County. For the first time in 40 years passengers trains were running again to Alloa. But the new line, built at a cost of more than £80 million, echoed the struggles of the Victorian promoters who constructed the original Stirling and Dunfermline Railway. The transportation of coal was the life blood of the Stirling and Dunfermline Railway (S&D) and coal is the main reason that line was re-opening in the 21st century. The original railway ran into a bitter legal row at Stirling which pushed up the cost and delayed the final link-up; similarly the new line ran well over budget and was a year late.

The men behind the S&D were speculators, caught up in the dying embers of the railway mania. Their plan was to build the line and, once it was up and running, sell it on to a larger company for profit. Their line was promoted in the late 1840s as a trans-Scotland highway at a time when Fife was almost isolated. Later in that century, both the Forth and the Tay would be bridged, but for the time being the Kingdom relied on ferry services and coastal shipping which made the transportation of goods and passengers slow and difficult.

The new line would link Fife to the Central Belt and then onwards through the expanding railway system to the great ports on the Clyde and to Liverpool. "There is no district in Scotland which more requires or will more certainly repay the benefit of railway communication than that embraced by the above line," said the S&D prospectus which appeared in *The Scotsman* on April 16, 1845.

There was a minor boom in railway promotion during 1836 and 1837 but it was not until the mid 1840s – when there was a return to affluence with good harvests in 1842 and 1843 – that there was a serious move to build a railway from Dunfermline to Stirling. Conditions were right. After a financial crisis in 1837, capital was again available, aided by the Bank Charter Act of 1844 and the Bank of England's increasing intervention in the money market.

The scheme was originally called the Stirling, Dunfermline and Queensferry Railway although Queensferry was dropped from the title to avoid confusion with another company. Branches were also planned from Alloa to Alva and from Alloa to Tillicoultry. It would require capital of £400,000 (£23,412,000 at 2007 prices)[1]. The company was offering 10,000 shares at £25 each, (£1,463.25) and suggested a return of 10 per cent.

In September 1845, James Anstruther, an Edinburgh advocate and Writer to the Signet, was appointed company chairman at a shareholders' meeting in Stirling.

Anstruther came from a landed family which owned 22,500 acres in Caithness and 2,100 in Fife[2]. The son of Col Robert Anstruther, of the Royal Tay Fencibles, he was born in 1803. The family home was at Balcaskie, Pittenweem in Fife.

The Anstruther family owned land in the East Neuk of Fife since the 12th century. They had many links with other landed families of the area, and sent many sons off to war as officers. Others went overseas as servants of the king and later to the British Empire, while others served as Lord Lieutenant or as an MP for Fife.

The engineer for the line was to be John Miller who, with his partner Thomas Grainger, had designed much of the early Scottish railway network. It was Miller who, in his early 30s, had full responsibility for the Edinburgh to Glasgow line, but who, in order to satisfy the English shareholders, was obliged to seek advice from time to time from prominent English engineers, who rubber stamped his plans.

The route of the proposed Stirling to Dunfermline line was across level country which the directors said "presented no engineering difficulties."

It was only intended to build a single line but powers would be taken to increase this to a double line "to accommodate the increase in traffic which may be reasonably calculated upon."

Figure 1. Alloa Station, c 1910. The station was rebuilt in 1885 by the North British Railway Company. It put right all the inconveniences and dangers of the original station. The remains of the derelict station were finally demolished in 1984. The new station was built a few hundred yards to the east of this building located on the old Alloa Brewery site. The new station has one platform and the building is unmanned. (*Picture: Clackmannanshire Council Library Services.*)

One year after Parliament passed the Act authorising the construction of the railway, S&D chairman Anstruther cut the first turf on the Dunfermline section in a field near Milesmark on March 8, 1847. The line was built in stages from the east, where the heaviest work was carried out, to the west where construction was expected to be easier. The first section, from Dunfermline to Oakley, was opened on December 13, 1849. The following summer, the railway reached Alloa and was opened on August 28, 1850. But it took another two years before the line reached Stirling, mainly due to a bitter row between two railway companies which resulted in two bridges being built, side by side, across the River Forth at Stirling.

The terms of the original Act stated that the S&D would be leased to the Edinburgh and Glasgow Railway (E&G) when it was completed. It was the usual practice for small companies to be taken over by larger ones. In fact, the growth of the Scottish railway network owes its origin to more than 200 small companies. In some cases the takeovers and amalgamations went through without a hitch but other companies were swallowed up by predators who were seeking to expand their operations and eliminate competition. At Stirling the S&D suddenly found themselves out of favour with the powerful E&G who used their influence with the local company, the Scottish Central Railway to block the Alloa line entering the royal burgh of Stirling.

The E&G took this action even although the 1846 Act authorising the building of the line gave the S&D running powers to form a junction at the north end of the Scottish Central's bridge over the Forth, and into Stirling Station.

The E&G refused to accept this agreement. Instead, they demanded not only a separate Stirling station but also a separate rail bridge over the Forth next to the one built by the Scottish Central.

Then, to complicate matters further, the E&G informed the S&D that they were not able to provide money to complete the line over the Forth into Stirling. The S&D directors pleaded that both companies would benefit from the savings "of a large sum of money which must otherwise be expended in building a separate bridge and formation of an independent station."[3] But their pleas fell on deaf ears. The S&D had fallen victim to railway politics.

A long and bitter court case followed and it was against this background that the section from Alloa to Stirling was opened on July 1, 1852. But with the access to the key bridge over the Forth denied, the S&D were forced to build their own at a cost of £20,000, which opened in August, 1853. There was no connection with the main line at Stirling and the S&D even had to construct a temporary station although the exact location is not known.

Later that year the E&G finally gave up their battle when the Lords ruled in favour of the Stirling and Dunfermline. Almost immediately, the E&G began to operate the line and within a few days negotiations were opened with the Central to make a junction at Stirling. The S&D now had their physical connection and their temporary station was closed, but the two bridges which

Figure 2. Two railway bridges cross the River Forth at Stirling. The one on the right was built to carry the original Stirling to Dunfermline Railway after the railway company which owned the other bridge refused them access. *(Picture: Author's collection.)*

Figure 3. Old Alloa station looking west. Alloa East Signal Box controlled the junction to the Devon Valley Line which leaves on the right. The main line to Dunfermline leaves Alloa on the lines out of the bottom of the picture while trains headed for Stirling had to pass through the station. At one time five signal boxes controlled the line between Stirling and Alloa. The entire new railway line is controlled by a signalman in Stirling Middle Signal Box watching over the trains using CCTV and other safety devices. *(Picture: Clackmannanshire Council Library Services.)*

still exist today remain a monument to the intense rivalry at the height of the railway mania.

The S&D became part of the E&G, which in turn was amalgamated into the North British, which later was one of the companies making up the LNER before nationalisation.

Alloa sat on the Stirling to Dunfermline line with branches to the harbour and Tillicoultry (both opened 1851). The line from Tillicoultry was later extended to Kinross to become the Devon Valley Railway, (opened 1871). There was also a branch running from Cambus to Alva (1863). Later the Caledonian Railway built the Alloa Swing Bridge at Throsk (opened 1889) which gave them limited access into what was now North British territory. The last piece of the jig saw was when the North British Railway Company opened the Kincardine branch linking Alloa to Dunfermline by the coast route (1906).

The transportation of coal was the lifeblood of the network and the principal mining operation in Clackmannanshire was the privately owned Alloa Coal Company. In the period before the First World War, much of their coal was exported from the docks at Alloa, Methil and Burntisland to Europe. The company also had collieries in the Bannockburn area of Stirlingshire. General Manager James Bain said at the time: "We have collieries at Alloa, Tillicoultry and Clackmannan, all connected with the North British Railway and at Bannockburn connected with the Caledonian Railway company. Our output is 400,000 tons a year from Alloa and 600,000 tons year from Bannockburn. We have 1,500 wagons of our own."

At the time of nationalisation, nine collieries were taken into public ownership. In the 1950s the National Coal Board (NCB) gave the go-ahead for the disastrous Glenochil mine (now the site of a prison) which operated only briefly between 1956 and 1962. There were also new mines at Solsgirth and Castlebridge which along with Castlehill and Bogside, fed into the Longannet Power station, Britain's second largest coal-fired power station.

As late as 1950 a new marshalling yard was built near Cambus and in 1960 there were proposals to modernise Alloa Station, but in the later 1960s the railways became casualties of the national closure of rural lines. The last passenger train ran from Alloa to Stirling on October 5, 1968. The Alloa-Kincardine Junction closed in the 1980 but the coast railway serving Longannet escaped the cuts.

As local supplies became exhausted, an attempt was made to exploit coal under the River Forth near Airth. After experiencing difficult geological conditions, Longannet mine flooded when a dam burst in 2002 and was subsequently closed.[4]

Even when the mine was working the power station had bought in coal from opencast sites in Fife and Ayrshire. Scottish Power had also imported supplies through the Hunterston deep water terminal on the Clyde and trains took the coal across Central Scotland to Longannet. Now, these supplies had to be increased to fill the gap.

The route took the trains through Ayrshire, Paisley, Coatbridge, Polmont and Linlithgow and across the Forth Bridge. At Townhill, the track layout requires the class 66 to perform a run round of the train. This requires the loco to uncouple from the front and then make its way to the rear where it re-couples before taking the train in the direction it has just come for a short distance to join the Longannet line.

Re-opening the Alloa line would allow these trains to decrease the journey time by about 90 minutes to three hours, and avoid the Forth Bridge. The new route would free up slots on the bridge for more passenger trains from Fife, and allow the coal trains to carry a greater payload – about 1300 tons compared with about 856 tons.

Alloa would also get back its passenger services and become reconnected to the national rail network for the first time since 1968. While politicians and railway experts argued at one level, a Back on Track campaign was launched at a local level to get the Wee County re-connected to the rail network. In fact the same arguments that had been put forward in an attempt to prevent the line's closure to passenger traffic in 1968 were now put forward as reasons for it to be re-opened to passenger traffic. Clackmannanshire Council, and its predecessor Clackmannan District Council, had been successful in preventing any development taking place that would have jeopardised the future re-opening

Figure 4. The scene at Alloa on May 15, 2008 as *The Great Marquess* arrives at the head of the special train to take part in the official opening. *(Picture: Ian Lothian.)*

by getting the line safeguarded officially in the 1986 Local Plan.

In July, 2004 the campaigning paid off when the Scottish Parliament gave the go-ahead for the project, estimated to cost £37 million. Legislation to re-open the Stirling-Alloa Kincardine line was the first railway bill to be approved by MSPs and the last bill to be voted at the Parliament's temporary home – the General Assembly of the Church of Scotland – before moving to their new controversial home at the foot of the Royal Mile.

Transport minister Nicol Stephen said then: "The rail link is expected to open around the end of next year, providing enormous benefits for the communities and economy across central Scotland."[5] Although work started in January 2005 Stephen was widely optimistic in both costs and the time taken to complete the task.

The 13 mile line would follow the old S&D route for Stirling to Helensfield, near Clackmannan, and then branch off on to the former North British line to Kincardine and Longannet. It would be single tracked with passing loops. To avoid confusion, it was given a new name, the Stirling-Alloa-Kincardine Railway (SAK).

The main contractors were First Nuttall, a partnership between Edmund Nuttall Ltd, experts in heavy civil earthworks, roads, bridges, etc and First Engineering, responsible for the railway work such as track, signalling and telecommunications. Among the tasks involved were:

- Remediation of old shallow disused mine working around the Kilbagie area. The technique used was called grouting – holes are drilled into the voids and then thousands of gallons of liquid grout are pumped in and allowed to set solid.
- Refurbishment of the three span Forth Viaduct. This was the bridge which the S&D were forced to build to give them access to Stirling.
- Removal of the old bridge deck at Helensfield near the village of Clackmannan and replacing with a new structure.
- Construction of a new railway station for Alloa.
- In addition to the construction of the railway, the project included the construction of the new Alloa Eastern Link Road.

The management structure was multilayer. Clackmannanshire Council, who had been the driving force behind the Bill, were the clients. Management consultants, Transport Initiatives in Edinburgh were brought in to manage the work, First Nuttall did the construction and feeding into this were the views of Network Rail who would eventually take over the line, and the train operators, and other interested bodies.

By June 2007 – two years into the project - it was clear the governing structure was not working and the Scottish Government decided to take over day to day management of the project through Transport Scotland, the national transport agency for Scotland which had been formed in 2006.

The project was severely criticised by Audit Scotland[6] over spiralling costs and poor management although they did note there were significant improvements when Transport Scotland took control.

The spiralling cots and delays have been put down to –

- The cost of remediation of old mine workings was much more than expected.
- The replacement of automatic half barriers with full barriers at Cambus level crossing, at the insistence of Health and Safety, resulting in added costs and a six month delay.
- A six month delay in the demolition of a bonded warehouse which stood in the path of the Eastern Link Road.
- Compensation for land was greater than expected.
- Lack of skills. The last time a railway had been built was in British Rail days and the knowledge base had become diluted.
- The uniqueness of the project which was costed on a design and built basis as many assumptions had to be made.

By the time the project finished, there was an impressive list of key figures:

- 1.3m man hours.
- 22,630 m plain line track and cable troughing.
- 33,846 rail sleepers.
- 79,094 tons of ballast.
- Three public level crossings (Waterside, Blackgrange and Cambus).
- Three private level crossings (Manor Neuk, Manor Powis and Kincardine).
- 29 signals.
- 29 Automatic Warning System units.
- One superstructure (the Forth Viaduct).
- 13 underbridges.
- 19 overbridges.
- Four footbridges.

Thousands of people flocked to the new Alloa station on Thursday, May 15, 2008 for the grand opening. A special train took VIPs and later local people and enthusiasts on trips to Stirling. The train was hauled by K4 class 61994 *The Great Marquess* from Alloa to Stirling, and returned hauled by preserved Deltic diesel 55 022 *Royal Scots Grey*, using carriages from the Scottish Railway Preservation Society.

Scottish Transport minister Stewart Stevenson was among the 300 guests who travelled on the inaugural train. He acknowledged that there had been difficulties with the re-opening of the line but he said: "This is a vital new link which will provide improved education and employment opportunities for communities across central Scotland, promote inward investment and increase sustainable economic growth to the area. This project has not been without its challenges, but we should celebrate a great day for the people of Alloa who can now look forward to much improved rail connections."

Coal trains are scheduled to use the new route this winter. Transport Scotland said they have worked with English, Welsh and Scottish Railways (the largest rail operator in Britain), and Network Rail to incorporate the Stirling-Alloa-Kincardine railway into a timetable that meets EWS's objectives. The spokesman added: "EWS has now confirmed acceptance for incorporating the SAK route in the winter timetable starting in December and a robust timetable has been agreed."

So the line which earned its living through the unglamorous job of shifting coal has been brought back to life for the modern coal trains. Alloa is also benefiting. New developments have sprung up around the station area and the introduction of a passenger service has given the town a much needed boost. Even although the pits have gone coal once again is king.

• David Bytheway is writing a book, Back on Track, which tells the history of railway network in the Alloa area, from wagon ways to their rebirth. The book is due to be published around Christmas. It is being produced in association with Clackmannanshire Field Studies Society with the financial support of Awards for All.

ACKNOWLEDGEMENTS

Thanks to Susan Mills, Clackmannanshire Council's Heritage Officer, Transport Scotland, First Nuttall, Alan Simpson, Hamish Stevenson and Ian Doig.

Reference

[1] National Archives, currency converter. Available at: www.nationalarchives.gov.uk/currency Accessed: November 1, 2007.

[2] Bateman, J. 1883. *The Great Landowners of Great Britain and Ireland,* reprinted Leicester, 1971, p 11.

[3] *The Scotsman,* September 29, 1849. p 4.

[4] Oglethorpe, M.K. 2006. *Scottish Collieries,* Royal Commission on Ancient and Historical Monuments of Scotland, Edinburgh.

[5] *Wee County News,* Alloa. July 9, 2004.

[6] *Stirling Observer,* July 2, 2008.

SIR JOHN MURRAY OF THE CHALLENGER EXPEDITION: FOUNDER OF OCEANOGRAPHY
People of the Forth (16)

Roy and Cathy Sexton and Ken Mackay

Introduction

In 1986 Stirling officials were lobbied to support a campaign to have Sir John Murray commemorated on a Canadian stamp. Few recognized him as the father of oceanography nor were aware of any local connection. Sir John had been born in Canada in 1841 but came to the Bridge of Allan to complete his education at the home of his maternal grandfather, John Macfarlane. It was the grounding he received at The High School of Stirling and as curator of his grandfather's museum that set him on the path to becoming one of the early twentieth century's most distinguished explorer-scientists. In later life he stated "It is always with emotion that I look down the valley of the Forth from Abbey Craig or the terrace at Coney Hill and see stretched before me the scene of my first explorations, my first scientific observations and my first collections".

Murray (Figure 1) together with Sir Wyville Thomson of Linlithgow guided the destiny of the Challenger expedition (1873-76), the greatest oceanographic exploration of all time. By unlocking the secrets hidden beneath two-thirds of the earth's surface the expedition could justifiably claim to have rivalled the great voyages of da Gama, Magellan and Cook in its contribution to our knowledge of the planet. Murray gave us the term oceanography and established Scotland as the international centre of this new science. He also placed the country at the forefront of world limnology (study of lakes). In this he received invaluable help from his life-long friend Laurence Pullar, the owner of the Bridge of Allan and Ashfield dye works. Their bathymetric study of the Scottish lochs would warrant the authors a place in Scottish history in its own right (Duck, 1990).

Although in 1986 there was an embarrassing lack of local recognition of Murray's contribution to science there was no shortage of international acclaim. Indeed his head had already appeared on a Christmas Island stamp (Figure 2). He was awarded knighthoods in Britain, Prussia and Norway. In Britain he won the prestigious gold medal of the Royal Society and the Founder's medal of the Royal Geographical Society, in France the Cuvier Medal, in Germany the Humboldt medal, in America the Cullum medal and in Australia the Clark medal. He was also awarded honorary degrees by the Universities of Edinburgh, Oxford, Harvard, Jena, Geneva, Christiania (Oslo), Toronto and Liverpool. He had named after him: an expedition, a research vessel, a deep sea trench, a bird, a bat, several fish, a spider crab, an octopus and several protozoa. Murray's acquaintances also claimed to recognize him in Conan Doyle's character Professor Challenger of *The Lost World* and much more recently the *Challenger* spacecraft was named after the expedition.

Belatedly in 1987 Stirling Council acknowledged its famous son naming a road in his honour, yet unfortunately there are still few who have heard of him. The purpose of this article is to enhance local recognition. There has been no comprehensive biography of Murray and this general account has been constructed from secondary sources which have specialized in different aspects of his eventful life.

John Murray's Life in Bridge of Allan

Born in Cobourg, Ontario in March 1841, John was the second son of Robert Murray, an accountant and his wife Elizabeth nee Macfarlane, who had emigrated there in 1834. He was probably named after his grandfather John Macfarlane who was born in Stirling in 1785 and who was to play a pivotal role in his later life. John Macfarlane left to work in Glasgow aged 14 and developed a talent for textile design. Between 1817-1845 he lived in Manchester and made his fortune as a major developer in the commercial heart of the city. He retired to Bridge of Allan in 1848 and while living in what is now the Old Manor established a new settlement in the area around Coneyhill at the eastern end of the village. His plans included twelve villas, a terrace of workers' houses, shops and an impressive museum (Allan, 2006). Macfarlane became a local philanthropist giving money towards the building of the High School of Stirling and providing Stirling's first Free Library. According to his obituaries he was also the first to suggest the erection of a monument to Wallace on Abbey Craig.

John Macfarlane was used to getting his way and family accounts suggest that Robert and Elizabeth Murray emigrated because he disapproved of their marriage. We know little of John Murray's early life except that he received schooling in London, Ontario and at Victoria School in Cobourg. It seems that his father died and his grandfather offered to complete his education in Stirling. In 1858 at the age of 17 he crossed the Atlantic to live in Bridge of Allan, joining many other members of his mother's family including two great aunts and Major John Henderson of the Westerton Estate.

It was the reputation of the High School of Stirling for navigation that determined John Murray's presence there. He learned about the principles of the sextant from an inspirational physics teacher Duncan Macdougall. In an address to the High School in 1899 he related how his courses in physics and geology were to be very influential in his subsequent career. Similarly during an interview with Bridge of Allan's *Spa Magazine* (AWD, 1899) he stated "I commenced my geological studies at the 'Bridge' and became enthusiastically interested in the subject through the exhuming of a whale at Cornton and an Irish Elk at Stirling Bridge. I took great delight in washing the clays of the carse for minute organisms and examining the shell beds in the banks of the Allan". He related how he traced the marks of glaciers over the slopes of the Ochils and from all these observations endeavoured to form a mental picture of conditions in the Forth Valley in bygone ages.

It seems that John Macfarlane always had plans for a museum or art gallery at Coneyhill both to attract new residents to his development and to act as a tourist attraction for the Spa. As his grandson's interest in natural history developed he saw it could provide a curatorial career for him. The recent discovery of John Macfarlane's 1860-3 letter book at the Natural History Museum in London has provided much new information about the establishment of the Macfarlane's Museum of Natural History as it was called. This it turn resulted in a re-evaluation of the importance it played in Murray's path to a distinguished career (Deacon, 1999).

The construction of a three storey museum was started about 1860 on high ground above Coneyhill terrace. Macfarlane had moved with his grandson from the *Old Manor* into *Edgehill House*, one of his new villas just across the road from the Museum. Murray became the curator with responsibility for purchasing, arranging and cataloguing the exhibits. He also provided some of the shells and birds' eggs from his own local collections. Macfarlane was very much the controlling hand being in weekly correspondence with an old Scots friend Thomas Brown a taxidermist and the curator of the Manchester Natural History Museum. To help provide the background in taxonomy and organisation of exhibits Murray was sent to the British Museum (Natural History) in London and the Jardin des Plantes in Paris. Macfarlane was determined that the museum was to be second only to the British Museum in its collections of quadrupeds, shells and birds. To this end examples of stuffed lions, tigers, leopards, giraffes, elephants, kangaroos, hippos, llamas, flying squirrels, alligators, crocodiles, armadillos etc. were collected. Malcolm Allan's recent entertaining account gives much more detail of the project (Allan, 2006).

At the age of nineteen Murray established a lifelong friendship with Laurence Pullar who eventually lived round the corner at *The Lea*, Kenilworth Road. Pullar had moved to Bridge of Allan from the family company's base in Perth in 1858. As a mechanic he arrived to help his brother John rescue the Bridge of Allan and Ashfield dyeing works which were threatened with closure. After twelve years "unremitting toil" the business proved very successful and Laurence became a wealthy co-owner. Pullar (1910) relates that "during the whole of the sixties there was hardly an evening when he and Murray did not meet for reading and the study of science". It was not all study though and Pullar was the president of Airthrey Spa Bowling Club from 1860-66 and Murray a champion bowler.

At the age of 77 Macfarlane's health began to fail and he found difficulty coping with his youthful grandson. As a consequence John moved to stay with Elizabeth Macfarlane his great aunt who lived next door at *Upperhill House*. Pullar (1910) relates that Murray was "tired of his want of a definite occupation and enrolled at Edinburgh University in 1863 where he studied medicine amongst other things." This only lasted a few terms because "his grandfather objected to his proceeding further with these studies". In his will of 1865 John Macfarlane set out a settlement for his grandson which he thought would provide him with a career and ensure the prosperity of the Macfarlane Museum. Firstly it required John to adopt the surname Murray-Macfarlane.

Then the will's trustees were *Directed to appoint John Murray to be curator of my Museum of Natural History declaring that the said John Murray shall be under their control and be obliged to perform any instructions given by them.* The trustees were charged with visiting the museum to check *that he has been in attendance every lawful day from ten o'clock until six o'clock in the evening.* For this John was to be paid £100 per annum and *Centrehill House,* Coneyhill was to be made over to him together with £150 to furnish it.

Most of Macfarlane's estate was left in trust to run and improve the museum. There is no reference in the will to his daughter Elizabeth Murray though his other Canadian grandson James Murray was included together with many other relatives. The will was subject to twelve changes which has made interpretation difficult for the modern Macfarlane Trust administrators. There was clearly disagreement between John and his grandfather and in 1867 codicil 8 cancelled the requirement to adopt the Macfarlane name. Then in a tenth codicil dated 4th September 1867 Macfarlane annulled the entire clause dealing with John Murray, essentially disinheriting him. This was apparently *in consequence of his having intimated to me that the considerable allowances with house etc. etc. as being too inconsiderable and that he could (do) much better in various other ways and that he intends to leave my service in October.* This left his grandfather's plans for the museum in ruins but as events unravelled Murray's prediction was to prove more correct than he probably imagined.

Freed from the constraints of his grandfather's regime the following February Murray shipped as the surgeon on the whaler *Jan Mayen* presumably on the basis of the medical lectures he had attended. They visited Spitzbergen and Jan Mayen Island eventually reaching 81°N. During the seven month trip he kept a log of the meteorology and made one deep-sea sounding at 160 fathoms (293 metres) measuring temperatures and retrieving mud from the sea floor. These were the first of many such measurements he was to make in his future career. Murray's grandfather's health deteriorated and when John returned to Scotland on 30th August 1868 he found his grandfather had died two days previously. He is buried in the Holy Rude cemetery with his father James Macfarlane, a Stirling merchant.

John Murray was later to become one of the Trustees of the Macfarlane's Trust who built the more elegant replacement Museum Hall on Henderson Street (formerly Macfarlane Street) in 1886. Later the old museum was demolished. Murray also mediated the transfer of books from the free library, firstly to the Smith Institute in 1882 and then subsequently to the Macfarlane Room in the Central Public Library in 1905. It was during the first of these transfers that he negotiated for the Stirling *Field Club* to be renamed *Stirling Natural History and Archaeological Society.*

According to Pullar (1910) "All his grandfather's trustees could promise John was a minute annual allowance for a short number of years". However together with his earnings from the whaler this seems to have allowed him to enrol again as a student at Edinburgh University and resume his informal studies. In his own words "I was sometimes known as a chronic student at

Edinburgh. I attended classes in nearly all the faculties but did not go in for exams and never took a degree. Robert Louis Stevenson ... with whom I worked in Professor Tait's laboratory used to say I was a wandering star for whom was reserved the blackness of darkness". At this time *RLS* was training to follow in the footsteps of his father and grandfather as an engineer.

During the next three years he lodged as a *student of science* in Edinburgh and experimented with the development of a deep sea electrical resistance thermometer in Professor Tait's laboratory. Weekends in Bridge of Allan were spent either with his great aunt or with Laurence Pullar. Whenever possible Murray and Pullar used to arrange dredging excursions on the Forth to study its marine biology. In 1870 they hired a 14 ton sailing yacht and sailed from Leith through the Caledonian Canal to Eigg and Skye to investigate the region's geology. During the trip they were invited for dinner aboard the yacht of the famous physicist Lord Kelvin who was obviously impressed by Murray's knowledge and later recommended him for the Challenger expedition.

During the fifteen years he was based in Bridge of Allan Murray fortuitously accumulated the skills that were to make him an ideal member of the forthcoming Challenger expedition. He was a proven seaman with practical experience of oceanography and a background in taxonomy and taxidermy. His experience of preserving, packing and transporting biological samples for his grandfather's Museum must also have been invaluable since wherever *Challenger* docked thousands of precious finds had to be sent back safely to London.

Sir Wyville Thomson and the Challenger Expedition

It was Sir Charles Wyville Thomson from Linlithgow who was to have an immense impact on John Murray's life. As a student at Edinburgh University Thomson became interested in marine biology whilst accompanying Prof Edward Forbes on dredging expeditions in the Firth of Forth. Forbes was one of the first oceanographers and is still remembered for propounding the theory that life could not exist in the *Azoic zone* at depths below 300 fathoms. Despite failing to graduate, Thomson progressed to become Professor of Natural History at Belfast where he took up dredging off the coast of Ireland. In 1866 he decided to visit Professor Michael Sars whose son had brought up a remarkable collection of unknown animals from depths of over 300 fathoms in the Lofoten fjords. One of these, *Rhizocrinus lofotensis,* was a stalked crinoid, a group previously known only as fossils. Thomson was impressed and his suggestion that we could be "still living in the Cretaceous epoch" unsettled the geologists.

As a result of his visit to Norway Thomson and the biologist Dr W. Carpenter persuaded the Royal Society to mount an expedition to explore the ocean deeps around the British Isles. The Navy offered their oldest paddle steamer which was rather inappropriately named *HMS Lightning.* They set sail from Oban in August 1868 and dredged down to 600 fathoms near the Faroes finding considerable life there. The next year a more appropriate survey ship

HMS Porcupine was provided and from it living organisms were retrieved from 2435 fathoms, nearly three miles beneath the surface. The presence of sponges, echinoderms, crustaceans and molluscs below 1000 fathoms should have sounded the death knell of the azoic theory though the topic remained controversial for some years. Many of these organisms were unknown and great excitement was generated amongst creationists by Thomson's prediction that deep sea animals identical to tertiary fossils would probably be discovered. As a result of the success of these expeditions Wyville Thomson was made an FRS and appointed Regius Professor of Natural History at Edinburgh.

This was the age of transoceanic telegraph cable-laying a science which in the UK was pioneered by Lord Kelvin in Glasgow. Much to Carpenter's consternation news had come that the United States, Germany and Sweden were all planning oceanographic surveys to aid cable laying. During a lecture at the Royal Institution in 1871 he called on H.M. Government not to let Britain's lead in marine science to go by default and appealed for them to undertake a thorough scientific study of all the oceans. Consent was given and in April 1872 preparations for the three-year circumnavigation of the globe began in earnest. A three masted, square rigged, steam corvette *HMS Challenger* which had been selected for the voyage (Figure 3) was placed under the command of Capt. George Nares from Aberdeen. Most of *Challenger's* guns were removed and she was refitted with laboratories and steam powered winding gear for deep sea trawls. Amongst the equipment stowed on board were 144 miles of rope for making bottom soundings, thermometers constructed to withstand the massive pressures in the ocean deeps, dredges for sampling bottom-living organisms and equipment for analyzing water chemistry. Wyville Thomson was to head the team of six scientists and he employed John Murray as a naturalist.

After an inspection by the Lords of the Admiralty and the Committee of the Royal Society, *Challenger* set sail on 21st December 1872. During the three and a half years she was away *Challenger* covered 68,890 miles surveying and recording depth, bottom deposits, chemistry, temperature etc. of all the world's oceans with the exception of the Arctic. The expedition revealed the ocean floor was far from flat and had trenches nearly as deep as Everest was high. In addition 4417 new species of marine organisms were discovered of which 715 were representatives of genera new to science.

The Nature of the Ocean Floor

Challenger started to investigate the nature of the deep ocean floor as she travelled from Tenerife across the Atlantic towards the West Indies. The initial bottom samples contained fawn *Globigerina* ooze which had earlier been shown to be principally composed of the remains of foraminifera. These are small (<1 mm) unicellular organisms which have an elaborate perforated shell made of calcium carbonate. Chalk rock was known to be composed of these shells and their discovery led to the proposal that chalk was still being formed on the sea bed. Wyville Thompson held the view that the ooze was composed of bottom-dwelling organisms but just before the expedition left it was claimed by

Major Owen that similar organisms were living in the surface layers of the ocean, suggesting the ooze was composed of their sunken dead remains.

To resolve this debate Murray deployed finely woven silk plankton nets at various depths in the water column. He discovered that the foraminifera in the upper 100 fathoms contained exactly the same species as those found in the ooze at the bottom. Initially Murray's data seemed to confirm Owen's theory but as the ocean got deeper a problem emerged. Sample by sample the ooze became progressively darker and eventually on 26th February 1873 at 3150 fathoms (3.5 miles) it was replaced by red clay with very little evidence of shells or calcium carbonate. Murray was still finding live *Globigerina* on the surface raising the question of why were there no remains on the bottom. As *Challenger* moved further west the ocean floor in the region of the Mid-Atlantic ridge came nearer to the surface and the *Globigerina* ooze reappeared only to be lost on March 7th as the water deepened again. Clearly some chemical process was occurring in water deeper than 3000 fathoms which was removing the shells. Buchanan the chemist pointed out that the concentration of carbonic acid increased with increasing depth which in turn would speed the rate of calcium carbonate dissolution. The depth at which calcium carbonate shells are completely dissolved is now known as the *Carbonate Compensation Depth*. Later Murray and Professor Renard of Ghent University were to demonstrate that the red clays which covered vast areas of the deep ocean floor were principally composed of the hydrated silicates of alumina and iron. They suggested these were derived from the decomposition of the pumice and volcanic ash deposited in the oceans and fine dust blown from the continents. The red clay was mixed with varying amounts of the remains of silicaceous organisms (diatoms and radiolarians) and microscopic particles composed of peroxides of iron and manganese.

The first deep ocean trawl for sea bed organisms at 3150 fathoms was accompanied by great anxiety since the extra hemp line needed to reach this great depth added another half a ton to what had already been strained lifting gear. When trawling at this depth the nets are dragged along the bottom at the end of a rope 8 miles astern. Although the operation was successful it was disappointing that nothing living was found. In March after passing over the mid-Atlantic ridge a second trawl at similar depth brought up sea worms and by the end of the voyage 161 species of animals had been recorded at depths greater 2500 fathoms. This proved a bit of an anticlimax since it had been suggested that organisms like trilobites, belemnites and gastropods which were only known as fossils might still exist in the deep ocean. After the trip had ended Murray concluded that there was no compelling evidence of a relic living fossil fauna, a great disappointment to the creationists. He proposed the less romantic notion that the deep sea had been colonized by migrations of organisms from shallower waters. By contrast with the low numbers of organisms at great depths huge numbers of organisms were recovered from the ocean floor when it was less than 1000 fathoms. For instance a trawl of 600 fathoms off Argentina recovered 500 types of invertebrates and fishes including 103 species new to science.

In the 10 months of her voyage *Challenger* made her way back and forth across both the North and South Atlantic before rounding the Cape of Good Hope and making for Antarctica. The first deep sea sounding in these cold waters was taken on leaving Heard Island (60°S) amidst much speculation amongst officers and naturalists about the likely nature of the deposit. Murray ventured that it would not be *Globigerina* ooze since he had not caught any in his tow nets for several days. Initially when a white coloured deposit was brought on board which resembled the globigerina ooze of the Atlantic it seemed he was wrong. Subsequent microscopic analysis revealed it to be primarily composed of the silicaeous skeletons of diatoms and had very few globigerina shells. It transpired that such deposits were a feature of cold circumpolar waters.

After the completion of the voyage, Murray, with the assistance of Renard divided these deep ocean floor deposits into either red clay or various oozes depending on whether the predominant organismal remains were foraminifera, pteropods (pelagic molluscs), diatoms or radiolarians. This classification has been adopted ever since. They were also able to map the distribution of these deposits since their own data was supplemented by the large numbers of samples (12,000) gathered over the next decade by vessels from United States, Germany, Monaco, Norway, France, Italy, Russia and Britain.

Challenger was the first steam vessel to cross the Antarctic Circle and in doing so she collided with an iceberg which could so easily have brought the trip to a premature end. Fortunately damage was light and the expedition sailed on to Australia, New Zealand and the Pacific Islands before visiting Japan and China.

Although the primary purpose of the expedition was to research the world's great oceans, *Challenger* spent more than half the time at anchor either in port or adjacent to the many remote islands she encountered. Terrestrial expeditions were mounted which also yielded a huge amount of information not only about the geology, fauna and flora but also the ethnology of the native peoples. Besides meeting kings, queens, and emperors they studied the native peoples including some who had only recently given up cannibalism. Both Captain Spry's (1876) and Eric Linklater's (1972) books deal in detail with these aspects of the voyage.

On March 23rd 1875 during the leg of the voyage between New Guinea and Japan *Challenger* made her deepest sounding of 4484 fathoms (5 miles) off the Marianas islands. It took 2.5 hours for the weight to reach the bottom and then to retrieve the line. The expedition was showing the ocean floor was no featureless plain and these trenches were nearly as deep as Everest was high. After leaving Japan *Challenger* zigzagged across the Pacific stopping at both the Hawaiian islands and Tahiti. The red clay deep ocean deposits found between Tahiti and Juan Fernandez were particularly interesting. One trawl on October 14th from 2385 fathoms brought up two bushels of manganese nodules together with 1500 shark's teeth and 42 cetacean ear bones. These had presumably settled there over countless millennia.

Eventually (much to the relief of the crew) *Challenger* left the Pacific and after navigating through the Magellan Straits during January 1876 made for Port Stanley in the Falklands. After a brief stop she sailed north to Montevideo, then to Ascension Island and St Vincent. The deep water temperature profiles mapped E-W across the southern Atlantic during the early part of the voyage had shown the eastern side was slightly warmer than the west. This led Captain Nares to suggest a ridge down the centre of the Atlantic keeping the two bodies of water separate. As *Challenger* sailed north the soundings showed the mid-Atlantic area was shallower than expected and the daring idea emerged that a continuous submerged mountain range might run down the centre of the Atlantic parallel to the continental outlines.

Challenger finally arrived home at Spithead on May 24th 1876. Queen Victoria conferred a knighthood on Wyville Thomson and by early July he and Murray were back in Edinburgh where their return was celebrated by a civic banquet. They brought with them 563 cases containing greatly in excess of 100,000 specimens which were distributed to 76 international specialists to describe. During the voyage Murray sent all his journals back to Pullar in the Bridge of Allan for safekeeping.

Murrray and the Edinburgh Challenger Commission

Before Thomson had sailed in *Challenger* he had negotiated a five year Treasury grant so that on their return the thousands of samples could be analyzed and reports written. It was agreed that the terrestrial items should be dealt with in London by the British Museum and Kew and the marine collections should be sent to the Challenger Commission Office in Edinburgh. Thomson employed Murray as his assistant for this mammoth task. There was a violent reaction amongst British scientists when it became known that Thomson intended to ship many of the samples to "the best men available irrespective of nationality". Duncan the President of the Geological Society was *howling mad* and an unpleasant public quarrel developed in which Darwin, Huxley and Hooker supported Thomson's position.

Initially everything went well and Edinburgh became the international centre for Marine Sciences visited by large numbers of leading biologists. The first of the expected Challenger Reports was published in 1880 but already serious difficulties were emerging with finance. The wealth of finds meant the authors were reluctant to constrain their publications and the costs of producing charts and illustrations got out of hand. Not all the press coverage was complementary and one newspaper commented that *we had got a lumbering volume of statistics for the monies spent feeding a mob of Germans and other aliens.*

Thomson had been very stressed during this period and suffered an attack of paralysis. It was clear that the work would not be finished in the five years and the Treasury gave no hope of renewal of the grant. Murray gradually began to take over affairs and Thomson died in March 1882. His role as leader of the Challenger expedition was commemorated by a magnificent stained glass window over the altar in St Michael's Church, next to Linlithgow Palace. It shows *Challenger* amidst a range of whales, sharks, corals and other sea creatures.

Following Thomson's death Murray was appointed to take over the *Challenger* Office and being a much more forceful personality he soon had five more years funding and relentlessly set about completing the task. The volumes of the Challenger Report started appearing more regularly and by the end of the decade all 31 zoological volumes were finished. The 31st volume was shipwrecked on its way from the printers to London prompting the Stationery office to pun hopefully that owners of the recovered volumes would forgive any imperfections *compensated by the knowledge that the polyzoa so beautifully figured in them, have been "drawn" from the bottom of the sea.*

Murray himself worked on with the Belgian geologist Abbe Renard, completing the volume dealing with the deep sea deposits in 1891. It largely confirmed the conclusions reached on the voyage. The hypothesis that the 50 million square miles of red clay on the ocean floor resulted from wind blown volcanic dust and denatured pumice was given additional credibility by the eruption of Krakatoa in 1883. Work on the Challenger Report was completed in 1895 with the final publication and world wide distribution of the 750 sets of the 50 thick quarto volumes (29,552 pages). Murray was responsible for several of them: the general narrative of the expedition, the volumes on deep sea deposits and those summarizing the results. The second five year Treasury grant ran out before this. In the end Murray himself financed the last volumes being reimbursed for their publication only when the final volume appeared. A *Challenger* medal (Figure 4) was struck which was presented to all the authors depicting a knight casting down his gauntlet as a challenge to the waters to give up their secrets.

Charles Darwin and the Great Atoll Controversy.

Seamen and scientists had long been fascinated by the beautiful circular coral reefs or atolls which seemed to spring miraculously from the deepest ocean floors. In the eighteenth century it had shown that the coral rock was principally composed of the accumulated limey remains of colonial sea polyps. These coral forming organisms were known to grow only in relatively warm, shallow (25 fathoms) water, posing the dilemma of how reefs formed where the ocean was thousands of fathoms deep.

Based on observations made during the voyage of the *Beagle* Charles Darwin proposed that fringing reefs initially developed around the shores of the exposed tips of extinct submarine volcanoes. He suggested the greater availability of the coral polyp's planktonic food on the reef's oceanic edge would cause the fringing reef to grow outwards creating a barrier reef with a large internal navigable lagoon. Then in regions where the ocean floor was subsiding the island would slowly disappear beneath the waves while the corals in the barrier reef would be able to grow upwards keeping pace with the changing sea level. In time a circular atoll would be formed enclosing an internal lagoon.

Although Darwin's theory was widely accepted there were over 400 known atolls and a few sceptics expressed surprise that the subsidence of oceanic floors was so widespread. In 1880 in a lecture to the Royal Society of Edinburgh Murray offered an alternative explanation (Murray 1880). Challenger surveys had revealed numerous extinct volcanic cones rising from the ocean bed some of which reached to within a few hundred fathoms of the surface. These were covered in *Globigerina* ooze and Murray argued that further deposition of foraminifera would slowly raise the submarine elevation to a point where it could be colonized by the reef forming corals. In common with Darwin's theory he proposed that once established the coral would extend seawards increasing the diameter of the reef. He envisaged that the atoll's lagoon would form not by subsidence but by the death of the central corals due to a lack of food, together with the dissolution of their limey remains by the carbonic acid in sea water.

Murray's theory generated little interest until the Duke of Argyll championed it in papers entitled *A Conspiracy of Silence* and *A Great Lesson* (Argyll, 1888). He pointed out that there was a reluctance to discuss the possibility that the great idol of the scientific world might be in error and argued that revered prophets could establish a sort of unconscious *reign of terror* suppressing derogatory opinions. He revealed that Murray had been induced to delay publishing his views for fear it might prejudice *Challenger* Office funding.

In 1896-8 an expedition financed by the Royal Society and the British Association set out to resolve the controversy by drilling a borehole into the reef at Funafuti atoll. The results superficially supported Darwin but were ambiguous. When interviewed for Bridge of Allan's *Spa Magazine* in March 1899 (AWD, 1899) Murray was obviously comfortable that the data verified his theory, as were many other oceanographers.

Britain's First Marine Research Station

While editing the *Challenger* Reports Murray felt the need of a marine station with access to sea water and aquaria etc.. He was helped by the Scottish Meteorological Society which in spite of its name had long been interested in Scottish fisheries. Murray offered to provide and equip the station if the society would donate £300 annually, to which they consented. Murray's friends and supporters raised £3000 in cash as well as apparatus and equipment. A notable donation was the steam yacht *Medusa* which was fitted out for oceanographic work. The boat was purchased with financial help from Murray's Bridge of Allan friend Laurence Pullar with design assistance from D. and W. Henderson's Clydeside boat-yard.

The site chosen was a flooded quarry at Granton on the Forth estuary which had originally been excavated well below sea level to provide stone for the harbour installations. The narrow wall of rock which kept the sea out was breached during a storm in 1855 flooding the quarry with sea water to a depth of 60 feet. In 1883 Murray took the lease with his friend Robert Irvine a chemist and director of a Granton printing ink company. An old lighter he named the *Ark* was moored in the quarry and converted into a laboratory with pumped sea water. He also took over a tannery, installing aquaria on the ground floor and a museum and laboratory above. Additional rooms in the ruined abbey on Inchcolm were furnished to accomodate any eminent visitors to Britain's first marine station. A staff of young scientists started work in 1884 under Murray's direction, their remit being to survey the fauna and hydrography of the Forth and the life history of food fishes. Murray and Irvine themselves investigated the secretion of calcium carbonate by marine organisms.

In the first summer *Medusa* was employed to investigate the herring shoals off the east coast but she was not sturdy enough for open water and in the autumn she was taken through the Forth and Clyde canal to work on the more sheltered west coast sea lochs (Marshall, 1987). Murray was looking to found a branch station on the west coast. He was persuaded by David Robertson, an eminent amateur naturalist and self made man, that Millport on the Isle of Great Cumbrae was the ideal spot. This proved the case and the *Ark* was soon to join *Medusa* drawn up into a sheltered inlet on the island where she remained for 15 years. As it was realised that the west coast was more fertile scientifically the main focus of station's work shifted to Cumbrae and Granton was closed in 1903. The quarry was filled and is now the site of a public park.

The idea of a permanent Millport Marine Station was pursued by Robertson who managed to raise enough money from Glasgow businessmen to build it. Murray opened the handsome building in 1897 presenting the *Ark* and her contents to the managing committee. The title Scottish Marine Biological Association was adopted in 1914 when a non profit making company was formed to promote research and education in marine biology.

It was also through his association with the Scottish Meteorological Society that Murray became secretary of a committee concerned with the establishment of a manned extreme weather station on the summit of Ben Nevis. The funds to build it were raised by public subscription and the station built to Thomas Stevenson's design was opened in 1883. Provisioned with enough coal and food to survive 9 months isolation the staff kept hourly records for 21 years. The stations' eventual closure, which caused considerable public disquiet, was ultimately delayed by a donation of £500 by Mr Mackay Bernard of Kippenross House, Dunblane.

Plotting the Depths of Scottish Lochs

Anybody who has used a Scottish Ordinance Survey map will be familiar with another of Murray's undertakings. His bathymetric surveys made between 1900-1909 still provide the information upon which the depth contours of most freshwater lochs are based. Apparently he became aware that little was known about the inland bodies of water when sailing through Loch

Ness in *Medusa*. His interest in the subject was further stimulated by Buchanan's finding (which he repeated) that Loch Morar was deeper (175 fathoms) than the ocean over the continental shelf. There had been much debate about the responsibility for surveying inland waters. In answer to a question posed in the House of Lords it was stated that it did not fall within the remits of either the Ordnance Survey nor the Admiralty. Murray wanted to organize systematic charting of all the Scottish lochs arguing that the information was important to water engineers and for the utilization of water power. In spite of support from the Royal Society the Government would not finance the undertaking. Never daunted Murray set about surveying the local lochs in the Teith catchments as a hobby. He had the practical and financial support of Frederick Pullar his old Bridge of Allan friend's son. Frederick designed the depth sounding equipment with which they charted 15 lochs including Katrine, Venachar, Voil and Lubnaig (Murray and Pullar, 1900).

On 15th February 1901 tragedy struck when Frederick Pullar (aged 25) died heroically trying to rescue skaters who had fallen through the ice on Airthrey Loch, now in the grounds of Stirling University (Gracie, 1994). Wishing to see his son's work finished Laurence Pullar offered £10,000 to complete the task and became a co-director of the enterprise. Three salaried officials worked from the Challenger Office supported by over 50 volunteers in the field. By the end of 1909 all 562 Scottish lochs had been surveyed and bathymetric charts produced. The reports which were dedicated to Frederick Pullar were published in six volumes from the Challenger Office. Those lochs that have been resurveyed using sonar show the information was remarkably accurate.

Science pays off. Wealth and the Annexation of Christmas Island

After failing to obtain government funding for so many of his projects it was with considerable satisfaction that Murray was able to announce in 1913 that "His Majesty's Treasury had received in hard cash … a sum greater than the cost to the country of the whole *Challenger* expedition" (Burstyn,1975). He was referring to the rents, royalties and taxes paid by the Christmas Island Phosphate Company which was set up as a direct result of his oceanographic investigations.

This venture arose out of Murray's interest in coral reefs. He wanted to know more about Christmas Island which was situated 190 miles SW of Java in water three miles deep. He had asked ex-Challenger officers Maclear and Aldrich whose vessels were deployed in the area, to gather rock for him. Chemical analysis suggested the island harboured valuable high grade phosphate deposits, which were in great demand as fertiliser to drive the agricultural revolution.

In 1888 Murray asked the government to annex this uninhabited island with the view to securing the exploitation rights for himself. After checking treaty obligations with the Dutch the Foreign Office dispatched Captain May of *HMS Imperieuse* to secure the island as a British possession. While the news of the annexation was awaited Murray had formed a syndicate of friends to defray the expense of further exploration. Dr Guppy a naval surgeon who had studied the geology the Solomon Islands was persuaded to lead the expedition accompanied by an experienced miner. They left in June 1888 two weeks after the annexation was announced.

The only way to get to Christmas Island was to persuade the owners of the schooner that sailed between Jakarta (Batavia) and the Cocos and Keeling islands to detour as it passed. The shipping company was owned by the Clunies Ross family who were descended from John a one time Shetland sea captain. He and his descendants had settled on the Keeling islands running coconut plantations with the aid of indentured coolies. Having agreed to land Guppy's party the boat sailed from Java to Cocos Keeling and back without dropping them off. While the very frustrated Guppy was on his way back to London, the Ross' attempted to establish a plantation on Christmas Island to reinforce their family's rival claim of ownership. During the next two years the claims on the lease were the subject of intense lobbying of the Colonial Office by both the Ross' agents and Murray. Harold Burstyn's (1975) account of this whole affair provides a fascinating read. Eventually in 1896 a joint company was formed.

Murray's first step before launching this massive mining effort was to commission a study of the island's wildlife by Charles Andrews of the Natural History Museum. To this he later added his own observations made during visits in 1900 and 1908. It transpired that there were several endemic species including a bat later named after Murray. They were also the first to observe the spectacular red crab migrations which are now considered one of the wonders of the natural world.

In 1899 mining began in earnest and eventually the Christmas Island settlement was populated by up to a thousand Chinese labourers. The size of the high grade phosphate deposit was estimated to be 12 million tons with each ton yielding £2 profit after shipment to London. A significant proportion of the rewards of this venture were used by Murray to support marine science. His chemist friend Robert Irvine also left his shares in the company to found the Edinburgh University Chair of Bacteriology.

Fame and a Tragic Death

In 1889 Murray abandoned bachelor life at the Caledonian United Service Club and married Isabel Henderson only daughter of Thomas Henderson owner of the Anchor shipping line. They may well have met when Murray was staying with her uncle John Henderson (1881 census) who helped design *Medusa*. After the *Challenger* office closed in 1895 the couple bought a large villa in Granton near the marine station which was renamed *Challenger Lodge*. Murray's collections were housed on the other side of the road in *Villa Medusa*. They had many important visitors including another enthusiastic oceanographer Prince Albert of Monaco who was able to berth his yacht there. Although his roots were now firmly in Granton Sir John did keep some contact with Stirling. For instance he addressed his old school (Graham, 1900), was interviewed for Bridge of Allan's *Spa Magazine* (AWD, 1899) and was honorary president of the *Stirling Natural History and Archeological Society* from 1903-14.

Murray was now a man of fame and influence and travelled all over the world taking his wife and young family (two boys and three girls) with him. In 1910 The New York Times carried a full page illustrated article entitled *John Murray seeks the secrets of the deepest seas. This noted English oceanographer now here tells of the curious and interesting animal and plant life in the ocean depths.* He seems to have been much in demand to deliver lectures, chair meetings and receive the many honours listed in the introduction. Snippets of letters to Sir William Herdman (Herdman, 1923), once a Challenger Office assistant, give an insight: "Tomorrow I deliver the Agassiz address at Harvard, but have been let in for the Lowell lectures (eight) and addresses here at Princeton … there was a dinner in our honour here (Washington) last night the British Ambassador was present … we go to Philadelphia Academy tomorrow then to New York … Osborn is to have 14 millionaires to hear me at the Museum as to what they should do for the study of the Ocean".

As early as 1885 Murray had been promoting a renewal of polar exploration. He judged that there was no great appetite for pure marine investigations but the public interest in the polar regions could be harnessed to provide useful oceanographic information. He was involved in the preparations of the *Scotia* or Scottish National Antarctic Expedition 1902-1904 which made a considerable contribution to marine research. William Bruce who led the expedition had spent time as a volunteer with Murray in the Challenger Office. In 1897 Murray also presented Fridtjof Nansen with a *Challenger* Medal in recognition of the oceanographic work carried out during his famous *Fram* expedition of 1893.

At the age of 69 Sir John's last major contribution to oceanography was an expedition with Johan Hjort round the north Atlantic in the Norwegian Fisheries research vessel the *Michael Sars*. Murray offered to pay all the expenses incurred on the 11,000 mile voyage. The expedition discovered a hundred new species including a massive 2 metre wide moonfish *Saccopharynx hjorti*. It is still the only specimen to have been caught and is preserved in Bergen museum. On their return the pair wrote the highly acclaimed text book *The Depths of the Ocean* (Murray and Hjort, 1912). Murray followed this with his last publication a little book in the Home University Library series *The Ocean; A General Account of the Science of the Sea* (Murray, 1913).

A few days after his 73rd birthday on March 16th 1914 Sir John was killed during the course of an afternoon spin in his new open tourer. The wheel at the time had been taken by his twenty year old daughter Rhoda, the chauffeur being next to her in the passenger seat. While changing gear on a clear straight road near Kirkliston the car skidded, mounted the embankment and rolled over twice. Sir John was killed instantly and Rhoda was knocked unconscious. To add to the tragedy Lady Murray was away at the time visiting their youngest son who was seriously ill at Eton. The funeral at Dean, Edinburgh was attended by representatives of all the scientific societies and public bodies with which he had been associated. Besides the family, the pall bearers included his lifelong friend Laurence Pullar and Admiral Aldrich from the *Challenger.*

In his will Murray left 1270 phosphate shares for oceanographic research. Initially this kept *Villa Medusa* running but after twenty years it was wound up and the books and records were sent to the British Museum of Natural History. The income was then used to fund the John Murray Expedition to the Indian ocean and after 1948 they financed the John Murray Travelling Studentships which benefited many young marine and freshwater biologists.

Bibliography

Early Life

Allan, M. 2006. The Macfarlane Museum of Natural History Coneyhill. *Forth Naturalist and Historian* **29**, 17-25.

A.W.D. 1899. Our local celebrity. Sir John Murray K.C.B. *The Spa Magazine* **8**, 4-10.

A.W.D. 1899. Sir John Murray's Address to the High School of Stirling. *The Spa Magazine* **9**, 11-17.

Deacon, M.B. 1999. A grounding in science? John Murray of the *Challenger*, his grandfather John Macfarlane and the Macfarlane Museum of Natural History at Bridge of Allan. *The Scottish Naturalist* **111**, 225-265.

Graham, J.L. 1900. *Old Boys and their Stories of the High School of Stirling.* Stirling: Eneas Mackay.

Pullar, L. 1910. *The Lengthening Shadows.* Published privately by Thomson, Dundee.

Watson, W.N. B 1967. Sir John Murray – A Chronic Student. *University of Edinburgh Journal* **23**, 1-16.

Role in oceanography

Argyll, Duke of. 1888. A conspiracy of silence. *Nature* **37**, 246.

Deacon, M.B. 1971. *Scientists and the Sea 1650-1900.* Aldershot, Hampshire: Ashgate.

Herdman, W.A. 1923. *Founders of Oceanography and their Work.* London: Edward Arnold.

Marshall, S.M. 1987. An account of the marine station at Millport. *Occasional Publication* **4**, University Marine Biological Station, Millport.

Murray, J. 1880. The structure and origin of coral reefs and islands,. *Proceedings of the Royal Society of Edinburgh* **10**, 505-518.

Murray, J. 1913. *The Ocean: a General Account of the Science of the Sea.* Home University Library **78**. New York: Henry Holt and Co.

Murray, J. and Hjort, J. 1912. *The Depths of the Ocean.* London: Macmillan.

Schlee, S. 1976. *A History of Oceanography.* London: Robert Hale and Co.

Challenger Expedition

Linklater, E. 1972. *The Voyage of the Challenger.* London: John Murray.

Spry, W.J.J. 1876. *The Cruise of HMS Challenger.* London: Sampson Low, Marston, Searle and Rivington.

Thomson, C.W. and Murray, J. 1880-95. *Report on the Scientific Results of the Voyage of HMS Challenger During the Years 1873-76.* 50 volumes. London: HMSO.

Bathymetric Survey of Scottish Lochs

Duck, R.W. 1990. The charting of Scotland's Lochs. *Forth Naturalist and Historian* **13**, 25-30.

Gracie, J. 1994. The men who plumbed the depths. *Scots Magazine* June issue.

Murray, J. and Pullar F.P. 1900. A bathymetrical survey of the fresh-water lochs of Scotland. Parts I-III. *Geographical Journal* **15**, 309-352 and **18**, 279-295.

Murray, J. and Pullar, L. 1910. *Report on the Scientific Results of the Bathymetric Survey of Fresh-Water Lochs of Scotland During the Years 1897 to 1909.* 6 volumes. Edinburgh: Challenger Office.

Christmas Island

Burstyn H.L. 1975 Science pays off: Sir John Murray and the Christmas Island phosphate industry 1886-1914. *Social Studies in Science*, **5**, 5-34.

Death and Obituaries

John Macfarlane *Stirling Journal and Advertiser* 4th Sept. 1868.
John Macfarlane *Stirling Observer and Midlands County Advertiser* 3rd Sept 1868.
Sir John Murray obituary by Kerr, J.G. (1915). *Proceedings of the Royal Society of Edinburgh* **35**, 305-317.
Sir John Murray killed in motor accident. *Scotsman* March 17th 1914.
Sir John Murray's career. *Scotsman* March 17th 1914.
Sir John Murray's funeral. *Scotsman* March 21st 1914.

Figure 1. Sir John Murray 1900. *(Courtesy of National Oceanographic and Atmospheric Administration Photo Library.)*

Figure 2. Sir John Murray commemorated on a Christmas Island stamp. *(Reproduced with permission of the Australian Postal Corporation. The original work is held in the National Philatelic Collection.)*

Figure 3. HMS Challenger under sail. *(Courtesy of National Oceanographic and Atmospheric Administration Photo Library.)*

Figure 4. The Challenger Medal designed by John Murray portraying a knight throwing down his gauntlet as a challenge to the ocean to give up its secrets. (© *National Maritime Museum, Greenwich, London.*)

STIRLING, GATEWAY TO THE NORTH:
I. ROMAN ROADS AND EARLY ROUTES

Ron Page

Introduction

'To pass in reasonable safety and comfort from southern to northern Scotland a man must cross the Forth within a mile or two of Stirling. Stirling is the brooch that holds together the two parts of the country' (Mitchison, 1970, 1, 2, quoting Alexander Smith, 1856). The head of the Firth of Forth, the area bounded by Stirling, Dunblane and Doune, is therefore the gateway to the north.

Two thousand years ago the land north of the river Forth seemed almost a separate country when viewed from Edinburgh. The estuary to the east of Stirling, called *Bodotria Aestuaria* by the Romans, was a considerable barrier to the boats of those times (Tipping and Tisdall, 2005). To the west were the extensive mosses of the carse land, difficult to cross except by the few trackways to and from the fords of the Forth and Teith. The importance of these ways across the mosses in remote times is shown by the presence of duns and brochs controlling access to them (Main, 1998, 2001). The low-lying carse lands on each side of the Forth are flanked by hills that impede movement. To the south are the Campsies, the Gargunnocks, and the Touch Hills, leaving only a restricted corridor towards the tidal limit of the river and the nearby fords. To the north the River Teith runs close below the hills. North of the Firth of Forth are the Ochil Hills, leaving only a narrow strip of passable land below the Abbey Craig, which then broadens out through Clackmannanshire to lead to the fertile lands which became the Kingdom of Fife.

When the Romans came they were funnelled by the geography of the land towards the river crossings near the site of the future Stirling. They were not penetrating a desolate wilderness. The country was well populated, and had been so for hundreds of years (Tipping and Tisdall, 2005). The remarkable density of Iron Age hill forts in the area, the Bronze Age burial cairns, and the even earlier megalithic standing stones testify to that. Whether the Romans came as conquerors, or came proffering client status to local rulers (Wilson 1997), as they seem to have done to the Votadini in Lothian, and perhaps also to the tribes in Fife, they headed towards the focal point that is now Stirling. Towards that point they built their main road from the south. That road much later became the Great North Road, and served to bring many an invading army to Scotland – William Rufus, son of the Conqueror, Edward I, Hammer of the Scots, and others after them.

When reading the following parts of this article, the reader will find it useful, even for those with intimate knowledge of the district, to have by them the appropriate Ordnance Survey sheets, either the Landranger 1:50 000 scale Sheet 57, or better still, the Pathfinder Series (1:25 000 scale) Sheets 365 and 366.

Roman roads

Two great Roman roads from the south converged on Elginhaugh, south east of Edinburgh (Figure 1). From the Roman Fort at Elginhaugh to the camps at Camelon, near Falkirk, most of the road has been lost, much of it obscured by buildings, or perhaps built over by modern roads. This Roman road pre-dates the Antonine Wall by at least half a century. From Camelon to Stirling the course of the road is well established, much of it clear on the ground, as for

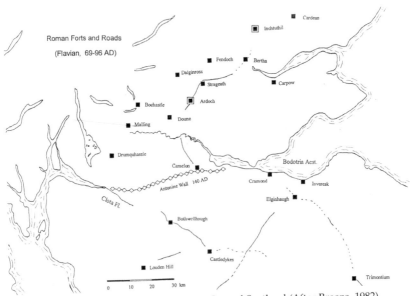

Figure 1. Roman Forts and Roads in Central Scotland (After Breeze, 1982).

example in Torwood, near Tappoch Broch. The Roman road then lies under the modern minor road to West Plean, heading towards the M9 roundabout at Bannockburn, then *via* St Ninians into Stirling: a description of this part of the road is given in the Royal Commission Stirlingshire Inventory (1963, 112-115). In Stirling itself the line of the road was recorded by Crawford (1925). Excavations in 1971, 1972 and 1974 by the Stirling Field and Archaeology Society, reported in *Discovery and Excavation in Scotland* for those years (pp 42, 40 and 65 respectively), confirmed Crawford's discoveries. The excavation in 1972 in the garden of No 6 Drummond Place showed a change of direction of the road 11° westward, and in 1974 a probable further 11° turn was reported.

Beyond Stirling for some distance the course of the Roman road has been lost. In 1792 the Rev. C. Tait read a paper to the Royal Society of Edinburgh (*Trans. iii, pt 2, 1794*) in which he described a road 'supposed to be Roman' (Maxwell, 1989, accepted it as Roman) crossing the Forth at Drip and extending about four miles to near the old Kincardine Church, about 300 metres SE and across the road from the present church. This may have been a road to Bochastle Roman Fort near Callander (Figure 1). There should in all probability be another road leading to the Ardoch Fort at Braco. A road leading north in that direction through the Keir estate was shown on Edgar's Map of 1745. A possible crossing place of the River Teith may be indicated by the field name of 'Broad Ford', near Ochtertyre. Excavations in the Keir estate by Professor St Joseph in 1975 and by Ron and Cathie Page in 1992 failed to find evidence of a road. Simpson and Allan (2000) probed the farm track 500 m east of Biggins Farm and found evidence of a well-engineered road extending some way south in the direction of 'Broad Ford'. Excavation would be required to show whether or not this is part of the missing Roman road, but it seems possible, even likely. It appears to connect to Baxters Loan, which passes below the Flavian marching camps south-west of Dunblane.

Further north the road was found in Kinbuck Muir and traced for 1.6 km towards Ardoch by J.S. Nicoll, manager of the Clydesdale Bank in Bridge of Allan. (*Discovery and Excavation (DES) 1971*) It is very unusual nowadays for a discovery to be made first on the ground, and then to be confirmed later by aerial photography, as this was (Maxwell, 1982).

Figure 2. Trace of pit beside the Roman road at Rough Castle, Bonnybridge. These pits are usually visible only in aerial photographs.

Near Glenbank aerial photographs revealed a series of pits beside the road (Figure 2). These pits are characteristic of Roman roads, dug to provide gravel for surfacing the road. This stretch of the Roman road leading south-westwards from Ardoch (Figure 1) is clearly aimed at the high point at grid reference NN 7805 0366 near Crofts of Cromlix, but has not been traced west of the B 8033 road. Whether it kept east of the river and passed through Dunblane as was believed by Barty (1944, 17), or on the other hand crossed the River

Allan and went either to Doune, where the Roman fort was excavated in 1999, or passed near the Flavian marching camps near Dunblane, remains to be seen. North of Ardoch the route of the road is well known and clearly marked on Ordnance Survey maps. It is particularly clear along the Gask Ridge (Figures 3 & 4, Woolliscroft, 2002), and the sites of the signal stations along the road there are well worth visiting: several are sign-posted and in the care of Historic Scotland.

Figure 3. Roman road, near Ardunie Farm, on Gask Ridge, showing the raised roadway (*aggar*).

Figure 4. Roman road along Gask Ridge, where it becomes the modern road near Gask House.

Historic roads

There was once a widespread misconception (e.g. Moir 1957, 101) that "After the Roman period no roads were made in Scotland until the seventeenth century, except for the occasional 'causeway'", a myth effectively disposed of by Professor Barrow (1984). Among his many examples of medieval routes he quotes the journey in 1304 of two carts carrying money for wages from York to Stirling, at least 83 miles of which were over Scottish roads. The journey took only seven days, a rate of over 30 miles a day. Edward II's baggage train on the way to Bannockburn in 1314 stretched for twenty miles along this road. Certainly this journey was in the main over the previous Roman road, but in the intervening 1000 years it must have been kept in repair, but by whom, and by what arrangements, we have no record.

Elsewhere, including north of the Forth, we read of the 'king's highway' (*via regis*), the 'public road' (*publica via, communis via, communis strata*), or the 'high road' (*magna strata, magna via*). These roads would seem to have been surfaced (metalled) roads capable of bearing wheeled traffic. There were other roads and tracks, often not surfaced, and less well defined. Drove roads, for example, would, at any rate in the hills, be wide and no more than a general direction decided by the topography. They would become more constrained as they entered cultivated country, and later, when enclosures became general, they were confined between stone walls. Many other tracks existed between settlements and key points, like fords across rivers. These tracks would vary in width from narrow footpaths to wider paths for packhorses, and still wider for sleds and carts. All would take account of the lie of the land, and seldom took a straight line between two points. Straight lines were characteristic of Roman roads (though by no means all Roman roads were straight), and later Military roads, but in the intervening period, especially during the time of the enclosures, estate roads laid out by the landowner were often as straight as the topography allowed.

In the medieval period upkeep of roads was a duty laid upon his lieges by the king, and we have little or no information about how this was devolved, as it must have been, to their tenants. After Royal power passed to Parliament the upkeep of roads (and suggestions to the Council for any new ones) was made the responsibility of the Justices of the Peace (*Acts of the Parliaments of Scotland*, 1617, 1641, and 1655). In 1669 an Act was passed extending the Statute Labour measures for upkeep of the roads, requiring heritors and cottars to provide labour on the roads (Harrison, 2005): later this service could be commuted to a money payment that could then be spent on waged workers. But the activities of the Justices of the Peace were insufficient, and even bringing in the Commissioners of Supply of the Counties in 1686 did not greatly improve matters. The condition of the roads continued to deteriorate, probably exacerbated by the increased use of those times. In the 1790s in the *Old Statistical Account* parish after parish registered complaints about the appalling state of the roads. In winter most roads were practically impassable, though this was being remedied by the institution of Toll Roads, each of which required a specific Act of Parliament. The scale of dues payable at the Toll was fixed, but the Toll Keeper had to bid at public roup for the right to collect them and he then retained the money collected. Locally, for example, on the road to Perth there was a Toll at Balhaldie, and another at Greenloaning. The Toll Keeper usually had a house with a projecting bay with side windows that allowed him to keep an eye out on each direction and on a joining road. Local examples have survived at Kilmahog, where the road to Brig o' Turk and the Trossachs meets the A84, and another may be seen at Port of Menteith where the road from Arnprior joins the A81. Tolls were abolished in 1879 (Roads and Bridges Act, 1878), and Local Authorities assumed responsibility for roads and bridges.

From Stirling north across the River Forth

In very early times the river was crossed only by fords. One at Stirling was between the present A9 road-bridge and the Old Bridge, and could only be crossed at low tide when the river flow itself was low. Another was 2 km upstream at Kildean, near the tidal limit of the estuary. This could be used much more often, provided that the river flow was moderate. The next crossing was at the Fords of Frew, 12 km west, but to cross here on the way north meant that the Teith also had to be crossed at Doune.

A bridge was built at Stirling at some unknown date, but certainly before the end of the reign of William the Lion (1165 to 1214): it was proudly depicted on the Old Burgh Seal (1296). This ancient bridge was destroyed after the Battle of Stirling Bridge in 1297, and although it was repaired in 1305 and 1336 it was replaced eventually by a ferry. In turn the ferry was replaced when the bridge now known as the Old Bridge was built in about 1415. It has been modified considerably since that time, but remains in its original position. Just upstream from the Old Bridge some massive masonry piers have been located under water and under the sandbank in the river. These appear to be the remains of the preceding ancient bridge (Page, 2001). From the Old Bridge, as before from the ancient bridge, the Causeway led north across what was swampy ground.

From the head of the Causeway a track led to the east along the flat land below Abbey Craig to Cambuskenneth and to Fife *via* Alloa. Another track climbed straight ahead up the steep slope towards Logie Old Kirk and Airthrey (Ethra was the early spelling) to the north (Mackay and Angus 1984: Figure 5). In earliest times the preferred route from Stirling to Dunblane would probably have been *via* Cornton. It is doubtful whether a road led west from Causewayhead towards Bridge of Allan because there was a swampy area near the present main entrance to the University, known as the 'Floris', created by an alluvial fan descending from a stream, the 'Rough Burn', which now feeds Airthrey Loch. A military road was taken that way in 1748 (see below), but that was after the bridge over the River Allan was built.

There was certainly an east-west road along the foot of the Ochil Hills: Logie Old Kirk occupies a very ancient site. There is reference to it in a charter of about 1178, but the presence in the graveyard of hog back tombstones of 10th-

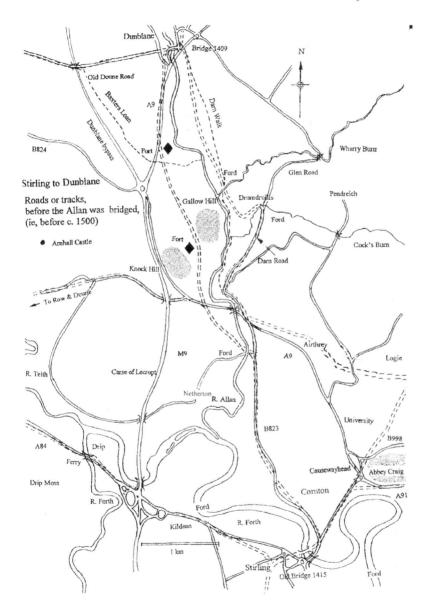

Figure 5. Old roads, shown as dashed tracks, on either side of the River Forth in relation to the modern road system.

11th century date (Figure 6) is evidence of an even earlier date (RCAHMS 1963, p 118).

Figure 6. Hogback gravestone (10th-11th century) in Logie Old Kirkyard.

Figure 7. Logie Old Kirkyard, showing sunken ancient lane below.

Eastward the track passed through Blairlogie and Menstrie, westward it went *via* the settlements of Airthrey and Westerton of Airthrey. This westward road through Airthrey originally ran to the south of the present narrow track between the Hermitage Wood and the wall around the University campus. Ralph Dundas, who owned the Airthrey estate before the Haldanes, diverted the road to the north from its earlier route, and greatly reduced its width, at some time after 1718 (Mackay and Angus, 1984). The early track passed from the Airthrey estate through Pathfoot village, then by Blawlowan more or less straight on to near the top of the present Coneyhill Road. All traces of the early road in this vicinity have been lost beneath houses erected there. It then formed the road leading to the bridge, before Henderson Street was set out. The road is preserved as the footpath that runs behind the property boundaries on the north side of Henderson Street (Figure 8). The plots have encroached quite some way on the original road width. The remnant of the road leading to the original bridge is now preserved by Albert Place. Before the bridge over the Allan was built, the road joined the Darn Road to Dunblane. These routes were typical of many, running along the lower edge of a slope above flat ground. It was therefore well drained, in contrast to the swampy ground below. Many other examples can be found in the district, a particularly clear example is on the north side of Flanders Moss.

Stirling to Dunblane before the River Allan was bridged (i.e., before *c*. 1500).

The town of Bridge of Allan obviously takes its name from the bridge. Before that bridge was built the area on which the present town stands was

Figure 8. Old road, now a footpath, above Henderson Street in Bridge of Allan.

known as 'Inneralloune' or 'Inveralloun' (spelling varied somewhat). It belonged to the Crown, and hence the rents of the cultivators were paid into the Treasury and recorded in the *Exchequer Rolls*. Inneralloun figured regularly in the *Exchequer Rolls* before 1523 as paying rent to the King: there are no references in the *Rolls* to Inneralloune after 1522. The village itself developed after the first bridge was built. Ella Maclean (1970, 7) suggests the bridge was built in 1520 but gives no source: the exact date remains obscure. The *Exchequer Rolls* give no indication that a bridge might have existed. In 1506 the *Rolls* (p. 719) record a Sasine of Inneralloun to Alexander Home. A Sasine was a record of property transfer, in this case a gift of land from the king to an individual. This would not mean the expulsion of existing farmers from their holdings, merely that rents would be paid to the new landowner. Fraser (1958) records several references to the 'lands of Inneraloun' (pp. 295, 296, 300, 310, 311, 366, 412, and 419). An involved dispute about ownership appears to have been resolved only in 1570 when the Stirling family acquired the whole of the lands (*Notarial Instrument of J Striuiling against Alexander Lord Hume*; p. 421), confirmed by the Testament of Sir James Striuiling of Keir, 9 December 1591. It seems likely that the bridge was built during this period, and some document giving the precise date may yet come to light.

In the early 19th century the discovery by Sir Robert Abercromby of a mineral well in his estate led to the development of the village of Bridge of Allan as a spa town (Maclean 1970). The Darn Walk was developed at some time in the second half of this century to add to the town's amenities. The relationship between the Darn Walk and the Darn Road is shown in Figure 9. The Darn Walk now leaves Blairforkie Drive and passes houses on the site of a paper mill, demolished in 1966. The paper mill had replaced a woollen mill and a saw mill. Beyond the houses the remains of a massive dam, now broken through, lie across the river. The start of the lade that led from the dam to the mill is still visible, though overgrown. Further along the path a small bridge crosses over the adit, or entrance shaft, to an old copper mine. There is a similar adit on the opposite bank of the river, and spoil heaps from the mine can be seen on the right in the field. (The main copper mine of Bridge of Allan is, of course, in Copper Mine Wood).

In the 16th century a journey from Stirling to Dunblane had the choice of two routes (Figure 5). A track branched from the beginning of the Causeway near Stirling bridge and passed westward through Cornton to Inneralloun, at that time open country. A ford near the present Bridge of Allan Fire Station allowed crossing of the Allan. From this ford one track led to Doune via Row (Figure 5 shows one possibility *via* Lecropt; another is *via* Netherton and Westleys: perhaps both existed). From the ford another track led north near the present A9 to Dunblane, probably passing through what is now the Closures and Plastics Factory, then by what would become the railway station, approximately along the present Station Road. It continued between Gallow Hill and the Iron Age fort that lies between Gallow Hill and Knock Hill (Figure 5). The route is marked on the 1:10 000 Ordnance Survey Sheet NS 79 NE as 'Old Military Road', but this is probably an error. It has not the appearance of

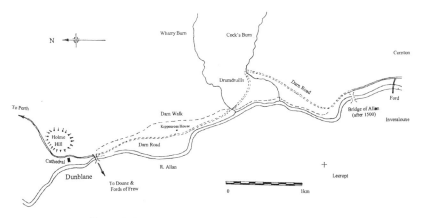

Figure 9. Darn Road and Darn Walk, Bridge of Allan.

a military road and seems to be much older. Near the Keir roundabout, Ordnance Survey mapping does not show its course but an aerial photograph taken by Dr David Woolliscroft in 2001 shows by a crop mark that it continues, to meet the A9 about 300 m north of the centre of the Keir roundabout. From there the earliest road, the military road and the A9 coincide, continuing past another Iron Age fort towards Dunblane. The early road, however, remained on the western side of the River Allan until it was able to cross a ford a little upstream from the present Dunblane bridge. That bridge has developed from one built in 1409 by Bishop Finlay Dermoch. (In medieval times it was usual for bridges to be built on the initiative of Bishops: other local examples are the packhorse bridge over the Knaik at Braco, and the bridge over the Machany Water, known as the Bishop's Bridge, on the way to Crieff, both built by Bishop Ochiltree in the early 15th century). Often the money to build such bridges was raised by the sale of indulgencies: one was promised a period of remission of the time to be spent in purgatory as punishment for one's sins).

Before the bridges existed over the Rivers Allan and Teith the preferred way to Dunblane from Stirling avoided the two fords by following the east bank of the Allan. It went along the Darn Road, past the Mill of Airthrey, more or less along Blairforkie Drive, along Glen Road until it reached the Cock's Burn where it swung west past Drumdruills and passing the Wharry Burn at the place where the present Darn Walk crosses this stream by the footbridge. The Meal Mill of Kippenross was beside the Burn near here, and the Darn Road went by this mill, following the east bank of the River Allan to pass in front of Kippenross House on the way to Dunblane. In 1858 the 'road called the Darring Road', by this time regarded as merely a footpath, was diverted by John Stirling of Kippendavie. Closing the road caused great local resentment. A wall was built across the road, but the work done by day was knocked down each night, allegedly by the same workmen (Barty, 1944, 269).

Bibliography

Barrow, G.W.S. 1984. Land Routes: the Medieval Evidence. In *Loads and Roads in Scotland and Beyond*. (ed. A. Fenton and G. Stell) pp. 49-66. Edinburgh.

Barty, A.B. 1944. *History of Dunblane*. Stirling.

Breeze, D.J. 1982. *The Northern Frontiers of Roman Britain*. London.

Crawford, O.G.S. 1949. *Topography of Roman Scotland*. Cambridge University Press.

Fraser, W. 1858. *The Stirlings of Keir and their Family Papers*. Edinburgh.

Harrison, J.G. 2005. Improving the roads and bridges of the Stirling area *c* 1660-1706. *Proceedings of the Society of Antiquaries of Scotland* **135**, 287-307.

Mackay, K.J.H. and Angus, D. 1984. Airthrey Roads: Captain Haldane's Magic Roundabout. *Forth Naturalist and Historian* **9**, 81-112.

Maclean, E. 1970. *Bridge of Allan, the Rise of a Village*. Alloa.

Main, L. 1998. Excavation of timber round-house and broch at the Fairy Knowe, Buchlyvie, Stirlingshire, 1975-8. *Proceedings of the Society of Antiquaries of Scotland* **128**, 293-418.

Main, L. 2001. *First Generations: The Stirling Area from Mesolithic to Roman Times*. Stirling.

Maxwell, G.S. 1982. *Discovery and Excavation 1982*. Edinburgh, 33.

Maxwell, G.S. 1989. *The Romans in Scotland*. Edinburgh.

Mitchison, R. 1970. *A History of Scotland*. London.

Moir, D.G. 1957. *Scottish Geographical Magazine* **73**, 101-110.

Page, R. 2001. The Ancient Bridge of Stirling. Investigations 1988-2000. *Scottish Archaeological Journal* **23**, 141-165.

Simpson, D.S. and Allan, T.M. 2000. *Discovery and Excavation 2000*. Edinburgh, 89-90.

Smith, A. 1856. *A Summer in Skye*. Edinburgh.

Royal Commission on the Ancient and Historical Monuments of Scotland. 1963. *Stirlingshire: An Inventory of the Ancient Monuments*. Edinburgh.

Tipping, R. and Tisdall, E. 2005. The landscape context of the Antonine Wall: a review of the literature. *Proceedings of the Society of Antiquaries of Scotland* **135**, 443-470.

Wilson, A. 1997. Roman penetration in Strathclyde south of the Antonine Wall. II. Romanisation. *Glasgow Archaeological Journal* **20**, 1-40.

Woolliscroft, D.J. 2002. *The Roman Frontier on the Gask Ridge, Perth and Kinross. An Interim Report on the Roman Gask Project 1995-2000*. Oxford.

STIRLING, GATEWAY TO THE NORTH:
II. ANCIENT, DROVE AND MILITARY ROADS

Ron Page

Dunblane to Doune and from Doune to the west

Before the Dunblane bridge over the Allan was built in 1409 by Bishop Finlay Dermoch, the river was crossed by a ford a little to the north of the site of the bridge. The old Doune road left Dunblane through what is now Bridgend. Part of the road is now lost where its route is replaced by the footbridge over the Dunblane bypass. It continues across a bridge at *Murdoch's Ford*, commemorating Murdoch, Duke of Albany, Earl of Menteith and Fife, beheaded in Stirling for treason in 1425 by James I. The road passes between Glenhead and Greenyards Farms as a road passable for farm traffic, though rough for cars. The old road then continues towards Dunblane as a well-defined track, now signposted as a footpath, with hedges on each side denoting its earlier width, until it meets the A820. A short distance west the remains of a bridge can be found. The old road then continued along the field boundaries and follows the northern boundary of the trees beside the B824. It crosses that road at the sharp bend, and on the far side of the road its track across the fields can be seen in favourable circumstances, after ploughing, as a stone scatter. The route then passes south of Old Newton House, and leads to where, before the Ardoch Bridge was built, there was a ford across the Ardoch Burn. A plaque on the bridge reads 'Built upon the Publick Expense of the Shire AD 1735' (Figure 2).

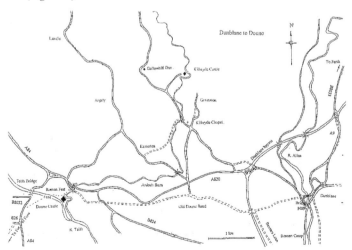

Figure 1. Old roads, shown as dashed tracks between Dunblane and Doune relative to the modern road structure.

Figure 2. Bridge over the Ardoch Burn at Doune.

Before 1535, when the bridge (Figure 3) over the River Teith south of Doune was built (by Robert Spittal, tailor to King James V) there was a ford near the Castle (Figure 1). This ford, immediately below the Roman Fort, would most probably have been used by Roman forces, and would have been an important factor in locating the Fort. From the ford a track led past the Castle: cars exiting from the Castle car park still use a part of it. The parish boundary along the Ashmill Burn leads directly to the ford, a sign of the antiquity of the route.

Figure 3. The Teith Bridge, south of Doune.

The now disused straight stretch of road leading from the junction of the B826 and the A84 towards Coldoch is part of an ancient route (Figure 1). It was shown on Taylor and Skinner's map of 1776 and was open until the 1920s: the late Mr Roy MacFarlane, whose childhood was spent in Doune, remembered being taken as a very young child along that road in a pony trap. This route south from Doune to the Fords of Frew would have been used by drovers heading south and seeking to avoid paying the toll at Stirling Bridge.

Figure 4. Road, now abandoned, leading south from Doune *via* Coldoch to the Fords of Frew.

Figure 5. Superbly constructed culvert under the abandoned road from Doune to the Fords of Frew.

The Glasgow to Perth route, from the Fords of Frew to Doune, passing Dunblane, is of great antiquity, suggested by the position of the Iron Age Coldoch Broch beside it. To control this vital route the Castle of Doune was sited beside it. The present Castle was built in the fourteenth century by Robert Stewart, Duke of Albany, but there was probably an earlier castle on the same site. There may indeed even have been an early medieval or dark-age fortification (a *dun*) there: the name Doune probably derives from this. The *Old Statistical Account* (1797) of Kilmadock or Doune by Alexander Macgibbon describes how 'The great roads from Edinburgh to Fort William, and from Glasgow to Perth, pass through this parish, crossing each other at the town of Doune. These roads are far from being in good order, but application is being made for making them turnpike. ... Except these two roads, there are no other roads, public or private, passable in bad weather'.

South of the old Doune road, beside the present Dunblane bypass, Baxter's Loan leads past the site of the Flavian marching camps to one of the mills on the River Allan (Figure 1). The name probably reflects the use of the track to take corn to the mill, but the track may be much older than the mill, and may even have served the Roman camps.

A road led west from Doune to Callander, subsequently upgraded to become part of the great Stirling to Fort William military road. Another went to the site of Old Kilmadock, with its ancient graveyard and church of St. Aedh, the focal point of the parish: Doune is in Kilmadock Parish and Doune was a dependent, a later development. The track joining Doune to its parent leaves the A84 just outside the village and its approximate direction can be followed beside the disused railway line and past Clarkton Farm. The last few hundred metres of track have been lost through ploughing so that the best way now to Old Kilmadock is by the path beside the Annet Burn, leaving the A84 opposite Burn of Cambus Lodge.

Several roads and tracks diverged to the north from the old Doune road. One went *via* Argaty and Lundie to the Braes of Doune. Two roads led to Kilbryde, meeting near Kilbryde Chapel. These roads, or their approximate modern equivalents, are still in use. A track that went from near Easterton Farm along the west bank of the Ardoch Burn, crossing the Burn at the site of the modern bridge by the Chapel, has fallen out of use but can still be followed, though with some difficulty. From the Chapel a road leads north to Grainston and used to extend further. Crossing the Burn, the road goes to Kilbryde Castle, a branch continuing past the recently discovered Gallow Hill Dun, past Nether Glastry, Dalbrack, the Judges Cairn (a Bronze Age burial mound), the Bows Farms, and so to the Braes of Doune. These roads were probably originally tracks used to gain access to shielings, summer grazing grounds for cattle. The remains of a large number (210) of these were discovered recently (RCAHMS, 1994). Some of these tracks may have extended through the hills to become drove roads, though they are not listed by Haldane (1997). The *Old Statistical Account* for Doune states 'The 2 (of six annual fairs) at Michaelmas and Martinmas are large cattle markets, little inferior to the famous trysts of Falkirk'.

Drove Roads heading towards Stirling Bridge

Cattle from the north and west, perhaps from as far away as Skye, crossed the Sheriff Muir on the way to Stirling Bridge and on to the tryst at Falkirk (Haldane, 1997). Drove routes can often be picked out by place names, such as Greenloaning, indicating where grazing was available, or Cauldhame, signifying a place of lodging, though rather primitive! The Sheriffmuir Inn represented superior accommodation. From the Inn there was a choice of routes to Stirling Bridge. One went south, close to the line of the present road, crossing the Wharry Burn near the present small bridge, itself quite old, and later dividing to allow descent either east by Logie Old Kirk or continuing south to Pathfoot. These routes are existing roads. An alternative *via* Pendreich remains as a track from the road between Stonehill Farm and The Linns to Pendreich Farm (Figure 6) where it continues as a made road dropping to Pathfoot.

This track was used by the fleeing left wing of the Government troops retreating from the Battle of Sheriffmuir. On their way to Stirling they used a bridge over the Cocks Burn built in 1708, just in time for their use.

Figure 6. Drove road across Sheriffmuir, from Pendreich Farm.

Drove roads were originally not clearly defined for most of their length, but as 18th century agricultural improvement extended enclosure walls, they became more and more confined. The track across the muir north of Pendreich Farm has been 'improved', and surfaced with stones. It is very straight and might be mistaken for a Roman road save that beside it at irregular intervals are roadstone quarries quite unlike the small pits found beside Roman roads.

Military roads

The London Government had been much concerned since 1688 over Jacobite support in Scotland, and continuing lawlessness in the Highlands. Matters came to a head with the Earl of Mar's rebellion of 1715. One consequence of the Battle of Sheriffmuir was the decision in 1717 to build a series of garrisons in Scotland, linked by military roads.

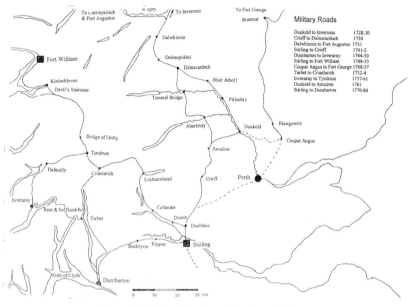

Figure 7. Military Roads leading from Stirling.

The initial plan was for four garrisons: Kilwhimen (later named Fort Augustus), Bernera, Ruthven, and our nearest example, Inversnaid. A road, planned by James Smith, 'Surveyor … in North Britain', was to run from Inversnaid *via* Glengyle, Balquidder, and Loch Tay to join, near Pitlochry, the Dunkeld to Inverness road, passing close by Rob Roy McGregor's stronghold at Inverlochlarig. The Chief Overseer at Inversnaid was Major Gordon, and Lieutenants Dumaresque and Bastide were in charge of the work on the road, which began in 1718. It was not completed, and is not traceable beyond Stronachlachar on the way to Glengyle. The Garrison itself was erected by 1719, in spite of a party of eight masons and quarriers being carried off by armed Highlanders (presumably McGregors) in August 1718. A plan of the garrison buildings is in the *Stirlingshire Inventory* (RCAHMS 1963, No. 112). The garrison buildings at Inversnaid can still be visited, though partly ruinous and partly incorporated into the buildings of Garrison Farm. The garrison at Ruthven, of similar plan, is preserved by Historic Scotland. The road towards Glengyle lies above and parallel to the modern road along Glen Arklet (Figure 8).

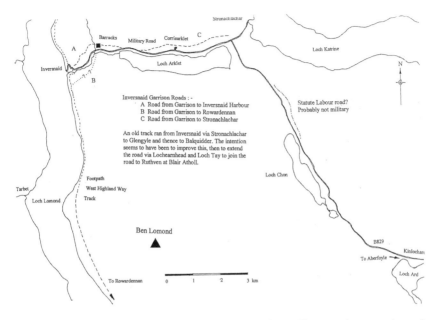

Figure 8. Roads to Inversnaid Garrison, part of the earliest military road system planned in Scotland after the 1715 rebellion.

From the garrison to the harbour the road is traceable over the hillside above the modern road descending to the Inversnaid Hotel. Presumably the garrison was supplied by boats. There is said to be a road from Rowardennan along the side of the Loch, along the line of the West Highland Way, but it seems likely that this was never completed: no trace of it is to be found. The present B829 road from Aberfoyle to Stronachlachar and Inversnaid is modern. Traces of an earlier road can be seen above the present road after passing Loch Chon (Figure 8). This seems to have been a Statute Labour road, but no record has been found to show exactly when it was built or when it was replaced by the present road.

The Inversnaid roads are not mentioned by Taylor (1976) because they predate what is known as the 'Wade era' from 1724 to 1740. The Glenshiel affair of 1719, an abortive attempt at a rising, was crushed by General Wightman when he captured three hundred Spanish soldiers who had landed. This alarm, coupled with a memorial sent by Lord Lovat to King George I in 1724 describing the unsatisfactory situation of lawlessness in the Highlands, gave rise to a Government Enquiry. As a result Major General Wade, MP for Bath, was sent to Scotland to look into 'the disarming of the Highlanders' and to suggest other remedies for 'good settlement of that part of the Kingdom'. General Wade stressed, among other proposals, 'the want of roads and bridges' to enable movement of troops and equipment to strong points such as Fort

William and Fort Augustus. He came to Scotland in 1725 as Commander in Chief, North Britain, armed with appropriate powers to bring about improvements. Wade began work on the military road system with the road from Fort William to Inverness. He realised that for access to the Highlands the two key towns were Perth and Stirling. But Perth had to be reached from Stirling, that 'brooch' bonding the north of Scotland to the south. For more than a century before Wade the Bridge of Allan had provided that vital link (see Part I: *Roman Roads and Early Routes*).

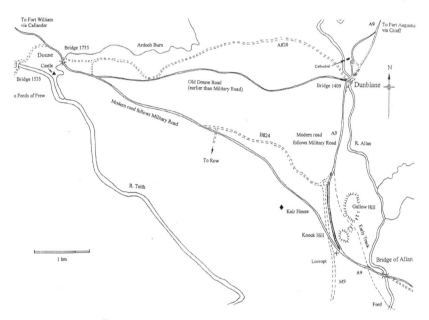

Figure 9. Military Roads through Bridge of Allan.

The early track from Causewayhead to Broad Loan and Logie (see Part I) was on too steep a slope for military traffic. Accordingly the military road was taken westward along the line of the present A9. Dunblane and Perth were already linked by an ancient road, the Roman road running along the Gask Ridge. It was used in 1715 by the troops of the Earl of Mar before the Battle of Sheriffmuir, resting the night before the battle at Naggyfauld by Kinbuck Muir. But this road was too rough and unsatisfactory for Wade, as was that from Perth to Dunkeld. Wade proposed first to link Dunkeld to Inverness, then to meet this road at Dalnacardoch by a road from Crieff, which could already be reached from Stirling (Figure 7).

Stirling to Crieff: 1741-2

The first efforts to build military roads were often unsatisfactory. Realignments and improvements to the Fort William to Inverness road, for example, had to be carried out in 1732. The existing Stirling-Crieff road had been assumed to be able to take military traffic but it was soon found, according to General Clayton, Wade's successor, to be 'in so bad a condition as to be in a manner impassable, and should there be occasion to march troops or carry artillery it would be impossible to do either'. As a result in 1741 the Commissioners of Supply for Perthshire received a petition from 'Major William Cawfeild' to be reimbursed because '… to make the road straight and more Commodious' he had had to pay £3 14s 6½d 'to the private parties'. The payment was evidence of the co-operation on road building between civil and military authorities in the Lowlands.

The Military Road to Crieff and then to Inverness had to go from Stirling over the Bridge of Allan. Both were upgraded from the existing Kings Highway. Stevenson (1723) in 'Macfarlane's Geographical Collections' (pp. 310-11): 'The Kings highway divides a little after passing the bridge of Allan, through this paroch one by Dunblain to Strathearn and Perth, the other by Doun to Menteth and the West Highlands'. It seems most likely that this division took place a short distance north of the present Lecropt church, close to where the A9 runs just above the M9: a track leads north off the A9 above the railway line which I believe to be an early track, a relic of the route from the ford across the River Allan (see Part I). The military road would most likely have run along the line of the present A9 into Dunblane: whether it passed through the town after crossing the bridge is not known. Caulfeild's road from Dunblane, ruler-straight like the previous Roman road lying between it and the River Allan, has now become the A9. At Greenloaning it turns across the river to Braco, then crosses the River Knaik at the Ardoch Bridge, heading straight to Muthill, diverging from the A822 as a minor road about 2 km from Braco. From Muthill it continues, again very straight, as the A822 to Crieff.

By 1742 Stirling was connected the whole way to Inverness by military roads. It was perhaps ironic that the first military use of these roads was by Jacobite troops retreating in 1746 to Culloden. Wade left Scotland in 1740. Caulfeild had served under Wade on road building and maintenance from 1732, and in that year he was promoted Major and appointed Baggage Master and Inspector of Roads. After the '45, in which he was Quartermaster to Sir John Cope, he became Deputy Governor of Inverness Castle, and usually then was addressed as Governor Caulfeild.

Military Road, Stirling to Fort William, 1748-53.

Like the military road to Crieff and then to Inverness, the Fort William road also had to pass from Stirling over the Bridge of Allan. A surveyor preparing for this military road noted 'From Edr. to Stirling and Down, to Kilmahug in Monteith is already carte road … Kilmahug begins the road, which is to be mended …' (Ruddock, 1974, 68). The road passed first through the Keir Estate, about 400 m north of Keir House, where its line is indicated on the Ordnance Survey maps. It converged towards the present B824, cutting across the road to Row 100m south of the B824, where a small trace of the military road remains as an entrance to the field (Figure 9). Soon after this the modern road and the military road coincide. At the sharp bend of the modern road, the military road met the old Doune road.

The military road continued to Callander, crossing the bridges over the Burn of Cambus, west of Buchany, and the Water of Keltie a mile before Callander. Beyond Kilmahog the route became more difficult. In July 1748 a warrant was issued 'upon the Storekeeper of Stirling Castle to Maj[r] Caulfeild or Mr Jas Campbell for such quantities of Powder as they may require for Carry[g] on the Road to Down' (Taylor 1976, 70). That summer thirteen miles of road were built from Stirling, but it seems unlikely that the gunpowder was needed for this stretch. In 1749, 300 men from Pulteney's regiment worked from Lochearnhead towards the Pass of Leny, and 300 of Sackville's regiment worked from the Pass of Leny towards them, work that would have found need for gunpowder to blast away rocky obstructions. Fifteen miles of road were made in that year, and the road was completed in 1753. In the main the modern road follows the course of the military road through the Pass of Leny and beside Loch Lubnaig, the military road diverging at Anie, traceable around the edge of the field and over the rising ground to rejoin the present road some distance beyond St. Bride's Chapel. Just beyond the chapel, above the modern road are the remains of an original, though partly collapsed, military bridge (Figure 10).

Figure 10. Bridge carrying the Military Road to Fort William, north of St. Bride's Chapel, Anie.

Stirling to Dumbarton, 1770-80

The earliest military roads in what is now Stirlingshire, as elsewhere in the lowlands, were built or improved from existing roads. This county also has the last of the military roads, that leading to Dumbarton. Major Caulfeild died in 1767 and work on the road was begun by parties of soldiers responsible to the Duke of Argyle (1771 to 1778) and continued under Lt. General Oughton (1779 to 1780). Slender details of its route are given by Taylor (1976, 69-70). The road left Stirling and passed through Cambusbarron, probably following the present Touch Road to join the A811 (Figure 11). About a kilometre further along the A811 its course can be seen to diverge behind Redhall Farm (Figure 12) and to join the minor road by Mains of Gargunnock into the village.

The military road continues to the west, crossing the Leckie Burn near Watson House. At Burntown there is a dogleg where the military road is crossed by the Glinns Road from Inch of Leckie Farm. Further west it goes over Boquhan Bridge, through Glentirranmuir to Kippen, and follows the B road from Kippen to meet again the A811 at Laraben. Through Arnprior the A811 displays the typical straight character of a classical military road. About a kilometre beyond Arnprior, near Garden, the military road diverges from the A811, continuing straight ahead, following the hedge line, being crossed at a dogleg by the minor road to Badenkep before passing behind Oxhill Farm into Buchlyvie. This section of the road apparently was scarcely used except by farm carts (revealed by excavation in 1989: Page and Page 1994). Soon after it

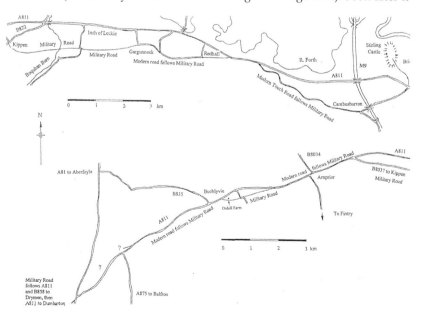

Figure 11. Military Road, Stirling to Dumbarton, 1770-80.

Figure 12. Military Road, now disused, near Redhall Farm.

was finished it was abandoned. Local users reverted to an earlier road, shown on Roy's Survey (1747-1755), that now forms the A811.

Conclusion

The maps in Parts I and II of this paper show how communications maintain continuity through the ages. Roman roads sometimes follow prehistoric tracks, and remain the foundations of many modern roads. Medieval tracks become drove roads or turnpike roads, and so on. Usually only Military Roads, Roman or post-1715, estate roads and modern bypasses break new ground.

Part I of this article *(Roman Roads and Early Routes)* drew the reader's attention to the use of Ordnance Survey mapping as a way of seeing the past. Throughout the two parts, emphasis has been on seeing the past on the ground, following and tracing these ancient roads across the landscape. Sometimes these old roads are now lost, sometimes they are seen only in favourable conditions or in particular lights. These and other roads remain to be explored, and new discoveries made.

Acknowledgements

I thank all those, too numerous to mention, who over the years have given advice and their opinions on these matters. I am particularly grateful to Malcolm Allan who made available to me a transcript of the Bryce Manuscript (1888), describing the roads and paths of Bridge of Allan, held by the Dr Welsh Trust. But in particular I must express my appreciation of the part played in this by my wife Cathie, who has walked these roads and paths with me, looked at the maps, and discussed the problems until we have reached these conclusions.

Bibliography

Macgibbon, A. 1791-1799. The Parish of Kilmadock or Doune. In *The Statistical Account of Scotland* XII: North and West Perthshire.

Haldane, A.R.B. 1997. *The Drove Roads of Scotland*. Edinburgh.

Macfarlane's Geographical Collections. 1723. Vol. 1. Description of the Parish of Lecropt in Perth and Stirlingshires.

Page, R. 2008. Stirling Gateway to the north: Roman roads and early routes. *Forth Naturalist and Historian* Vol **31**, pp.35-46.

Page, R. and Page, C. 1994. Excavation of a disused military road at Buchlyvie, Central Region. *Glasgow Archaeological Journal* **19**, 101-105.

Royal Commission on the Ancient and Historical Monuments of Scotland. 1963. *Stirlingshire: An Inventory of the Ancient Monuments*. Edinburgh.

Royal Commission on the Ancient and Historical Monuments of Scotland. 1994. *Braes of Doune: An Archaeological Survey*. Edinburgh.

Ruddock, T. 1974. Bridges and Roads in Scotland: 1400-1750. In *Loads and Roads in Scotland and Beyond*. (ed. A. Fenton and G. Stell) pp.67-91. Edinburgh.

Taylor, G. and Skinner, A. 1776. *Survey and Maps of the Roads of North Britain or Scotland*.

Taylor, W. 1976. *The Military Roads in Scotland*. Newton Abbot.

A NEW CHAMBERED CAIRN IN THE UPPER FORTH VALLEY

Angela Gannon

A new chambered cairn has come to light in the course of tree-felling operations in a plantation to the north-east of Loch Lomond. It was one of a number of monuments visited by officers of the Royal Commission on the Ancient and Historical Monuments of Scotland (RCAHMS) in the autumn of 2006 in response to a request from Lorna Main, Stirling Council archaeologist. Another was an unusual group of prehistoric carvings cut into an outcrop, including cups, a rosette and large ring-markings. The cairn was first discovered by Jim Ferrall, the Harvesting Work Supervisor with the Cowal and Trossachs Forest District of the Forestry Commission, whose attention had been drawn by two large capstones exposed after the area was cleared of trees. He had been searching for a covered well or spring that was known locally to supply the farm at Creityhall on the Buchanan Estates, owned by the Duke of Montrose. Having located this in the gully of the burn a short distance to the south-west, he realised that another explanation would have to be found for the two large slabs. Such was the importance of his discovery that a two-person team from RCAHMS revisited the cairn on a cold but bright November's day later that year, recording it by measured plan at a scale of 1:100 (Figure 1). This find is described and considered within its local and wider context.

Figure 1. Ian Parker (RCAHMS) undertaking a measured survey of the chambered cairn by plane table and alidade. One of the upright slabs is visible centre right, alongside the two capstones.

The cairn is situated in Garadh Ban Wood, an area previously planted with conifers, only a short distance from the Drymen to Balmaha section of West Highland Way. It lies towards the leading edge of a broad flat terrace between two burn gullies at about 170 m OD (NS 4522 9189), and commands fine views to the south-west over Loch Lomond and the row of islands that marks the line of the Highland Boundary Fault. The cairn is now reduced to little more than a low stony mound measuring 15 m from N to S by 12 m transversely and up to 0.5 m in height. The remains of the chamber lie off-centre to the south-west and comprise of two upright stones and two displaced capstones. Its overall plan, however, can no longer be determined, and the two upright stones are set splayed to one another; that on the W measures 0.53 m by 0.25 m and 0.15 m in height, and that on the E, which is heavily laminated, 1 m by 0.18 m and 0.8 m in height. The first of the capstones, its SE corner resting on the smaller of the two uprights, measures 2.1 m by 2.03 m and up to 0.3 m in thickness; two fragments are broken off at its NE corner. The second capstone lies immediately adjacent to the N, flush with the surface of the cairn, and measures 2.3 m by 1.7 m and 0.17 m in thickness. Small pieces of quartz lie scattered across the surface of the cairn (Figure 2).

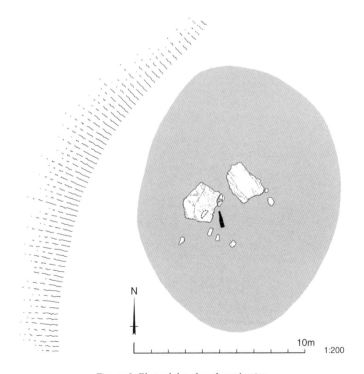

Figure 2. Plan of the chambered cairn.

The identification of the monument as a cairn is beyond question, and the size of the two large capstones argue for a chamber of Neolithic date rather than a cist of the Early Bronze Age. Geographically, the majority of Neolithic chambered cairns in the area belong to the Clyde tradition of megalithic building, a regional grouping that covers Argyll, the islands of Arran and Bute, much of south-west Scotland and up into Perthshire. Cairns of the Clyde group typically comprise a chamber defined by large stone slabs set on edge, often overlapping, sometimes subdivided into smaller compartments by septal slabs, and covered by a mound of stones and earth. In simple examples the covering cairn may be circular or oval, with access into the chamber only available from the body of the cairn and by the removal of a capstone, but in more developed forms, often of more than one period of construction, a series of large upright stones, arranged in a shallow semi-circle, define the façade of a forecourt in front of the entrance leading into the main chamber. Cairns elaborated in this manner tend to be trapezoidal on plan. Associated artefacts and the few radiocarbon dates that are available for this type of tomb, suggest that the Clyde cairns belong to the earliest phase of Neolithic monument building in Scotland (fourth millennium BC).

So where does the cairn in Garadh Ban Wood fit into this overall pattern? In terms of its surviving architectural detail, there is perhaps not enough visible evidence to place the cairn within the Clyde grouping, and only excavation can really provide the answer. Nevertheless, with capstones of such size, the monument is much more than a simple cist, and its oval shape and central chamber defined by thin edge-set slabs, slightly splaying and suggestive of an overlap, are in keeping with the more simple examples of Clyde-type tombs. As such, it provides us with a very welcome addition to the otherwise thin distribution of Neolithic funerary monuments in Stirlingshire, but one that has seen significant additions over the last thirty or so years.

The first of these new discoveries emerged in 1980 with the identification of a hitherto unrecorded long cairn at Edinchip, near Lochearnhead in Perthshire (Davidson and Henshall, 1984). This was followed in 1991 by the recognition of a chambered cairn at Auchenlaich near Callander, incorporated into the south-south-east end of an exceptionally long stony mound (*DES 1991*, 9). Then, in 1992, during the RCAHMS field survey of the area around the Braes of Doune, another four were found, three of which were identified as Clyde-type tombs (RCAHMS 1994, 6-8). More recently, in 2000, another Clyde-type chambered cairn was discovered at Carie during the RCAHMS Ben Lawers survey, undertaken in partnership with the National Trust for Scotland. In terms of the overall distribution of Neolithic funerary monuments, this steady trickle of new discoveries has helped to bridge the gap between the outlying group of cairns previously recorded in the glens of Perthshire and those examples in Argyll and the south-west. More tantalizingly, it holds the promise of yet more to come, particularly in areas covered by extensive forestry plantations that are now reaching maturity (Figure 3).

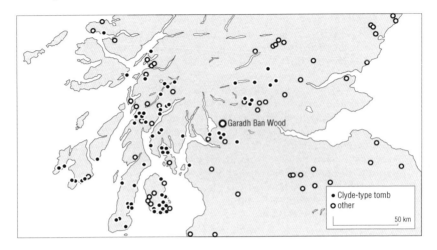

Figure 3. Distribution map showing the cairn in relation to Clyde-type tombs and other Neolithic funerary monuments.

A common feature of these cairns is their location on the fringes of the uplands, and in the case of the cairn in Garadh Ban Wood, its geographical position provides extensive and truly stunning views to Loch Lomond and further to the south-west. The paucity of comparative sites in the lower-lying ground can in part be explained by the intensity of later land use, reducing sites to little or no surface traces, but aerial photography is helping to extend the distribution of Neolithic burial monuments, supplementing the archaeological record with the discovery of at least two long barrows. One of these lies at Glenhead on the edge of a terrace to the south-east of the Ardoch Burn in Kilmadock parish, Stirlingshire, and while the barrow itself has been levelled by ploughing, the cropmarks of its flanking ditches are visible on aerial photographs. At Craighead, just across the border into Perthshire, a comparable pair of narrow ditches has also been revealed by aerial photography. No trace of a chamber can be detected on the aerial photographs of either, so it is not possible to claim that these are ploughed-out chambered cairns. It is perhaps more likely that these are unchambered long barrows, which are traditionally regarded as the typical funerary monuments of the eastern seaboard. When excavated, such barrows as that at Dalladies, Kincardineshire (Piggott, 1974), and more recently at Eweford West, East Lothian (Lelong and MacGregor, 2007), these have been found to cover timber mortuary structures, rather than stone-built chambers. Another timber mortuary structure was also found beneath the unchambered round mound at Pitnacree in Strath Tay, Perthshire (Coles and Simpson, 1965).

While fieldwork has been able to enhance the record of Neolithic funerary monuments in the fringes of the uplands, aerial photography is providing the equivalent for the adjacent lowlands. The RCAHMS programme of aerial survey, however, is contributing much more than this, for it has added significantly to the repertoire of Neolithic monuments in the lowlands, revealing mixed assemblages of round and long mounds, timber halls, mortuary enclosures and cursus monuments. Examples of all of these monuments are now known sweeping up into the Forth Valley. The two long barrows have already been mentioned, while the large circular mound at Tulloch Knowe, near Doune, may well turn out to be a round barrow of Neolithic date (RCAHMS 1979, 9, No. 29). A timber hall has now been excavated at Claish just outside Callander (Barclay, Brophy and MacGregor, 2002), while a pit-defined cursus monument has been excavated at Bannockburn (Rideout, 1997). What was once considered a rather barren area in Neolithic Scotland has been shown to contain a diverse range of circular, long and very long monuments. This contrasts with the uplands, where the monuments are largely limited to chambered tombs and decorated stones.

Geographically, central Scotland sits at the seam between these two zones. On the face of it this appears to reinforce the long-standing view that stone built monuments occur to the west and timber built monuments to the east. However, nothing is ever as simple and clear-cut, and the excavations in advance of an extension to a sand and gravel quarry at Upper Largie, near Kilmartin in Argyll, led to the chance discovery of a pit-defined cursus and a pit-defined enclosure, both monuments more typically associated with lowland Scotland (*DES 1997*, 19-21). In effect, we should anticipate that the lowland repertoire extends throughout the uplands. In this sense, the monument at Auchenlaich (see above), three times as long as any other known long barrow, is more readily interpreted as a bank barrow or cursus, providing an upland expression of a type of linear monument more commonly found in the lowlands.

The cairn in Garadh Ban Wood has not only added to the number of Neolithic funerary monuments within this part of central Scotland, but has also contributed towards a greater understanding of the early prehistoric settlement. That so many new monuments have been identified in an area that can hardly be described as remote, must surely beg the question of what others yet await discovery.

Acknowledgements

I would like to thank Jim Ferrall, Lorna Main and David Easton for bringing site to my attention and for an enjoyable day out together in the field; Ian Parker for planning the site with me and providing the illustrations; and Strat Halliday for his endless encouragement, help and advice.

References

Barclay, G.J., Brophy, K. and MacGregor, G. 2002. A Neolithic building at Claish Farm, near Callander, Stirling Council, Scotland, UK. *Antiquity* **76**, 23-4.

Coles, J.M. and Simpson, D.D.A. 1965. The excavation of a neolithic round barrow at Pitnacree, Perthshire, Scotland. *Proceedings of the Prehistoric Society* **31**, 34-57.

Davidson, J.L. and Henshall, A.S. 1984. A Neolithic chambered long cairn at Edinchip, Perthshire. *Proceedings of the Society of Antiquaries of Scotland* **113**, 35-9.

Discovery and Excavation in Scotland (DES).

Lelong, O. and MacGregor, G. 2007. *The Lands of Ancient Lothian: Interpreting the Archaeology of the A1.* Edinburgh.

Piggott, S. 1974. Excavation of the Dalladies long barrow, Fettercairn, Kincardineshire. *Proceedings of the Society of Antiquaries of Scotland* **104**, 23-47.

RCAHMS 1994. *The Royal Commission on the Ancient and Historical Monuments of Scotland: Braes of Doune: an archaeological survey* Edinburgh.

RCAHMS 1979. *The Royal Commission on the Ancient and Historical Monuments of Scotland. The Archaeological sites and monuments of Stirling District, Central Region* Edinburgh.

Rideout, J.S. 1997. Excavation of Neolithic enclosures at Cowie Road, Bannockburn, Stirling, 1984-85. *Proceedings of the Society of Antiquaries of Scotland* **127**, 29-68.

SCOTLAND'S RURAL PAST IN THE FORTH VALLEY

Tertia Barnett

Introduction

While many parts of the Scottish countryside are sparsely inhabited today, this pattern was established only within the last two centuries. Until the mid 19th century, and later in some areas, the vast majority of the population lived and worked close to the land. Thousands of abandoned buildings, overgrown walls, old field systems and enclosures litter the countryside and present eloquent reminders of this rural past. The wealth of archaeological material, especially that dating from the 18th and 19th centuries, is unparalleled in northern Europe and encapsulates a vital period of social change during the agricultural and industrial revolutions.

Despite the frequency of physical remains and documentary evidence for rural occupation during the later historic period, little is known about these settlements or the lives of the people that occupied them. Until recently, they have been considered of limited archaeological significance and have rarely formed the focus of serious academic study. The vast majority of sites are unprotected, and this marvellous material resource is deteriorating through neglect, the impact of construction work and the changing demands of modern land-use. There is now growing concern over the urgent need to locate, identify and document abandoned rural settlements across the country if we are to better understand this important part of Scotland's past, make it available for further study and help preserve it for the future.

The Forth Valley in later history

These concerns are no less true for the Forth Valley, which was extensively settled and farmed into the later historical period. The First Statistical Accounts record, for example, populations of 1865 for Port of Menteith parish in 1755 and of 1777 for Kippen parish in 1793. While a small proportion of the population was occupied as merchants, craftsmen or physicians, most people were farmers or farm labourers, working rented land to nurture a relatively meagre crop of oats, barley, potatoes and beans. Although industrialisation, especially in the weaving industry, had an early grip on this region (Shaw 1984), the farming way of life was slow to change. In the late 18th and early 19th century, improvements to the system of agriculture, such as more effective crop rotations, tree planting and the enclosing of fields, enabled many farmers to prosper (Devine, 1994). These developments, combined with the draining of the carse (Cadell, 1913) to reclaim rich soils for crops from beneath the mosses, raised the standard of living for some land-owners and farmers, at least temporarily. However, despite the relative affluence and longevity of farming in this area, very few of the farmsteads, townships or related structures such as kilns, grain mills and enclosures have been researched or documented in any detail, if at all. Again as an example, for the parish of Kippen there are no records of townships, and only six farmsteads and two mills documented in the national database of ancient and historic monuments, the National Monuments Record (NMR) curated by the Royal Commission on the Ancient and Historic Monuments of Scotland (RCAHMS). This seems unlikely to be a true representation of the density or distribution of settlement documented in the First Statistical Accounts (RCAHMS/Historic Scotland 2000).

Furthermore, the records in the RCAHMS database are brief in the extreme and provide only a cursory view of the evidence for and patterns of historic rural settlement. All the records in the NMR of farmsteads in Kippen were created in the years between 1995 and 2001 during recording by the RCAHMS for the First Edition Survey Project (FESP) (2002). The FESP project was developed to address the dearth of evidence on the ground for medieval and later rural settlements in Scotland. Information on all structures (for instance, farm buildings) depicted on the First Edition six-inch Ordnance Survey maps of Scotland as being unroofed, and features associated with these unroofed structures, was added to the RCAHMS database. As the First Edition Ordnance Survey maps were created between 1843 and 1878, they provide a crucial snapshot of a dramatically changing landscape and way of life. Over 25,000 townships and farmsteads with abandoned buildings were recorded across Scotland by FESP, representing over a fifth of all known archaeological sites in Scotland. Although their locations and cursory information drawn from the First Edition maps have been added to the RCAHMS database, very few such sites have actually been visited to check if the locations and brief records are accurate, and only a handful have been archaeologically surveyed in any detail. Many more rural settlements remain undocumented, either because they were abandoned after the creation of the First Edition Ordnance Survey maps, or because they were already in an advanced state of ruin when the area was mapped during the 19th century, and were not thought worthy of record.

A typical entry (this one for Arngibbon farmstead in Kippen, NMRS number NS69SW 29) reads:

> *Arngibbon*
> A farmstead, comprising one unroofed L-shaped building and one structure is depicted on the First Edition of the OS six-inch map (Perthshire 1866, sheet cxxxvi & cxxxvii), but it is not shown on the current edition of the OS 1:10000 map (1979).

Entries such as these add valuable data to the distribution map of rural settlement (Figure 1), but tell us little about the history of the farmstead or the varied fortunes of its inhabitants. Because many farms in the Forth Valley appear to have been relatively prosperous as a result of the 18th and 19th century improvements, it is perhaps likely that few buildings were unroofed or abandoned at the time of the First Edition mapping programme (Figure 2), and so were not identified and added to the RCAHMS database during the FESP project, thus lacking even cursory entries. Consequently, we lack even very brief records for many of the rural settlements in this region.

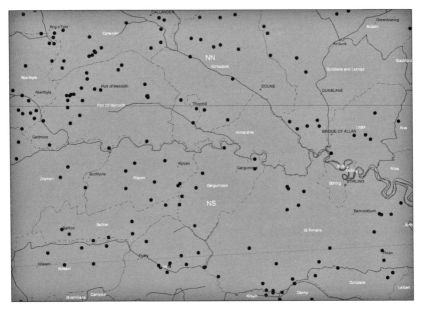

Figure 1. Map of part of the Forth Valley, including Kippen and Port of Menteith parishes, showing the distribution of FESP sites i.e. settlements that were recorded as being partially or wholly abandoned on the First Edition six-inch Ordnance Survey maps of Scotland dating between 1843 and 1878. (RCAHMS ArcGIS plot of FESP sites)

Scotland's Rural Past project

Building on the results of the FESP project and following the initiative of the Historic Rural Settlement Group, a research organisation comprised of academics and heritage agency representatives, a partnership between RCAHMS, the Heritage Lottery Fund, Historic Scotland, the National Trust for Scotland, and Highlands and Islands Enterprise launched the Scotland's Rural Past project (SRP) in October 2006 to address this gap in our knowledge.

Based at RCAHMS in Edinburgh, a team of four staff has been recruited to run the SRP project until September 2011. The aims of the SRP project are chiefly to work with local people of all ages to investigate, record and raise awareness of medieval and later rural settlements across Scotland and so improve our current knowledge of rural history and elevate the conservation value of the archaeological remains.

Through a programme of training and support, the team enables groups and individuals to develop their own projects which focus on investigating and recording local sites of interest to them, and researching the history of the area and the lives of past rural communities. The majority of projects are fieldwork based, but volunteers are also encouraged to explore historical

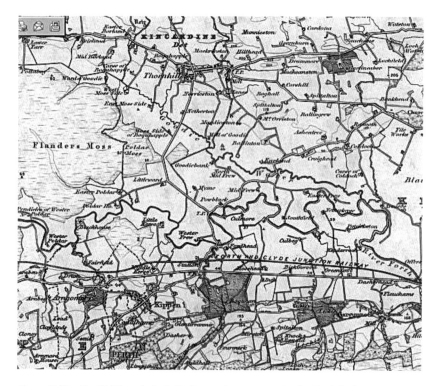

Figure 2. The First Edition six-inch Ordnance Survey map for the Forth Valley (1860-1863) depicts a more densely populated, ordered and improved landscape around Kippen, with scattered settlements interconnected by a complex of roads and the Forth and Clyde Junction railway. (National Library of Scotland)

documentary evidence, and to raise awareness of their findings more widely through publication and interpretation initiatives. In tandem with adult members of the community, the SRP team also runs an education programme with schools and Young Archaeologists Clubs across Scotland. The SRP project aims to develop and complete at least 40 projects with local communities and 15 projects with young people by September 2011.

Sharing ideas and forging partnerships

The SRP team has enjoyed a very busy time since the project was launched in October 2006. The popularity of the project with local communities across Scotland has far exceeded expectations, and is still gathering momentum in 2008 as it becomes more widely publicised. It provides an exciting opportunity for people to develop their interests with the benefit of expert support and advice, and a context for sharing their ideas and results with other like-minded people. As the number of projects grows, new links between groups and communities are being forged, and valuable new partnerships are taking shape. This can be true for local communities in the Forth valley.

The end of the first year of SRP was celebrated in October 2007 with the launch of the project website www.scotlandsruralpast.org.uk. The website has been designed to be a valuable resource for anyone wanting to find out how to get involved with the SRP project, and contains extensive practical advice and guidance on how to set up a project, carry out historic research and undertake archaeological survey of rural settlement remains. The website enables all volunteers who are participating in SRP projects to publicise and discuss their findings online. A specially designed electronic form, accessed through the website, allows trained volunteers to submit their digital records, photographs, site sketches and detailed plans directly to the RCAHMS database after validation by the SRP team. These records in turn become publicly accessible through *Canmore*, the RCAHMS web-based database.

Sharing skills and expertise

Fieldwork to survey and record rural settlement remains lies at the heart of SRP. To encourage all communities and individuals to develop fieldwork programmes, the SRP project provides training for all volunteers. The SRP team is able to draw on the immense depth of expertise within RCHAMS in order to build skills and confidence with local groups (e.g. Figure 3). The demand for training has been overwhelming since the project started. The original target of completing 19 training courses during the five years of the project has been exceeded within the first two years. At the time of writing this article, the team have completed 25 two-day courses, and one week-long course on Arran in partnership with the National Trust for Scotland. In total, over 400 volunteers have so far received training.

The majority of SRP training courses are fieldwork based, covering a range of survey and recording techniques from identifying and interpreting rural settlement remains, to creating detailed site plans and records. In most cases, the training provides exactly the right catalyst for groups and individuals with an existing interest to develop their own fieldwork projects. Following volunteer demand, the SRP team has also developed a new two-day course focusing entirely on research into historical documents. This course helps volunteers to learn where to access archives, old maps and aerial photographs, and how to use them effectively to interpret the fluctuating history of rural settlements. This course is now being run twice a year and has had a very enthusiastic response. At present, it is run from RCAHMS in Edinburgh, but the intention is to work with local libraries and archives in other regions.

Breaking new ground

At the time of writing in September 2008, 40 separate local projects have been initiated, of which seven have been completed. Further projects are due to start by the spring of 2009. Volunteer projects are spread across Scotland and vary in size and ambition. At one end of the spectrum, dedicated amateurs

Figure 3. A group of volunteers explore a crofting township overlying a pre-improvement settlement at Naast in Wester Ross with experts from RCAHMS as part of a typical SRP two-day training course (copyright RCAHMS).

with considerable archaeological experience from the North of Scotland Archaeology Society (NOSAS) are making a detailed record of all the rural settlement remains along the length of Strathconon. When completed, this project will have researched and made detailed records of over 60 previously undocumented archaeological sites and will have rewritten the history of an entire glen. At the other end of the spectrum there are a number of smaller groups with more limited archaeological experience, but with boundless enthusiasm and aptitude. Many of these groups have taken on more modest projects, at least initially, such as researching and recording the histories of single farmsteads and townships. To develop a better understanding of and regard for land-use and settlement history over time, volunteers are encouraged to be aware of all aspects and traces of rural life. This can result in unexpected and exciting spin-offs from rural settlement – one SRP group on Mull recently identified the remains of an early Christian chapel near Tobermory, entirely unknown until their work. Staff from RCAHMS are working with the group in October 2008 to make a detailed record of the site, which will also feature in a forthcoming BBC Radio Scotland broadcast.

SRP has had particular interest from groups in and around the Cairngorms National Park. Here, projects have been set up investigating settlements in Glen Clova, Strathavon, Glen Clunie and Glen Feardar. Another is under development with the Balmoral Estate ranger service to record and interpret a township at Spittal of Glenmuick and shielings in the surrounding hills.

Several projects are also underway in Argyll and Bute and in the Highlands, and a number of projects have recently begun in the Lowlands, especially in Dumfries and Galloway. This year interest in SRP is spreading even further and projects are already established on Skye and in the Western Isles, while in 2009 the SRP team hopes to work with volunteers on Shetland and Orkney in partnership with local organisations.

Given the historical and archaeological potential of the Forth Valley, there are many valuable opportunities here for detailed study. Two projects only are currently running in the whole of Perthshire and Stirlingshire, and there is ample scope for a further project, or projects, aimed at improving our understanding of rural settlement in this area. Archaeological fieldwork and research by local historian John Harrison and the RCAHMS (2001) in Menstrie Glen in the Ochils, and by the RCAHMS in the Braes of Doune (1994) both demonstrate what can be achieved through such an approach. Surveys of these areas identified a considerable number of prehistoric to post-Medieval structures for which no previous record existed: the identification of the rare remains of possible medieval homesteads in the Braes of Doune was a particularly exciting result of this work. The surveys also provided the opportunity to study the history and morphology of the pre- and post-Improvement steadings and shieling sites, of which little was known previously. Such studies change our perceptions and drive research forward; SRP provides the means for wider contributions to this process.

Raising awareness

The Scotland's Rural Past project is not just about building an accurate and well-researched record of rural settlement. Inspiring more people to take an interest in local history is key to improving understanding and appreciation in both the short-term and the long-term. A number of SRP volunteer groups are encouraging other members of their communities to learn more about their rural heritage through local events based on their projects, including guided walks, 'hands-on' days, talks and exhibitions. For example, the Heights Heritage – a community-led project on the Heights of Keppoch between Dingwall and Strathpeffer – held an event in September 2007 during which over 60 adults and children worked together to create a drawn record of a deserted croft settlement which had been researched in detail by members of the group. The results of their work were put on display in the village hall alongside photographs and anecdotal records of what life had been like on the Heights in the past. This successful idea has now been adopted by other SRP groups. Elsewhere, some groups, such as the newly formed Strachur Local History Society, have even started running their own training sessions for other members of the community, based on the skills they acquired during the SRP training.

Looking forward

As the SRP project takes shape, the team is developing new ideas for training and expanding local skills. A partnership with woodland experts is raising exciting opportunities for exploring the landscape legacy of historic woodland management, while partnership with the Forestry Commission aims to improve access to sites on the Forestry Estate as part of the Year of the Homecoming in 2009. In November 2008, the SRP team is holding its first annual conference at the Birnam Arts and Conference Centre in Dunkeld. This promises to be an exciting opportunity for volunteers and professionals from across the country to get together and share their results through talks, discussions and displays, and to talk more informally during the conference dinner and site visits.

As the SRP team becomes more involved with volunteer groups across the country, it is clear that the real aims of the SRP project are being achieved – a high standard of work being submitted to the RCAHMS database, often from people who have little or no previous experience; real enthusiasm and growing capacity in the community; new initiatives emerging to raise awareness more widely; and engagement of the younger generation. Further details about the Scotland's Rural Past project can be found on our website or by contacting the team at srp@rcahms.gov.uk. We would be delighted to hear from readers of the *Forth Naturalist & Historian*.

References

Cadell, H.M. 1913. *The Story of the Forth*, Glasgow.

Devine, T.M. 1994. *The Transformation of Rural Scotland*. Edinburgh.

RCAHMS. 1994. *Braes of Doune: an archaeological survey*. Edinburgh.

RCAHMS and Historic Scotland. 2000. *The Historic Landscape of Loch Lomond and the Trossachs*. Edinburgh.

RCAHMS and Historic Scotland. 2002. *But the walls remained: a survey of unroofed settlement depicted on the first edition of the Ordnance Survey 6-inch map of Scotland*. Edinburgh.

RCAHMS. 2001. *Well sheltered and watered: Menstrie Glen, a farming landscape near Stirling*. Edinburgh.

Shaw, J. 1984. *Water Power in Scotland 1550-1870*. Edinburgh.

DUNBLANE WEATHER REPORT 2007

Neil Bielby and Malcolm Shaw

Introduction

It is with regret that we must record that the University meteorological station at Parkhead is probably dead. After refitting with new automatic recording features in 2004 it offered the prospect of being able to monitor the weather of Stirling semi-automatically with an increased number of parameters, including hourly measurements of temperature and of sunshine becoming available. The availability of a set of normals established over the 30 years (1971-2000) made its use very attractive. The station last recorded useful data in 2006.

It seems to have been a problem of vandalism and failing power supply – batteries, or was it just our expectation that "automatic" meant "maintenance free".

The 2007 weather report has been prepared from data taken from a private recording station in Dunblane. Data from this station has been used before whilst Parkhead was off line.

Neil Bielby has recorded the weather in Dunblane since 1995 and all averages etc. refer to the last 13 years. The Parkhead normals figures are included after the Dunblane 13 year averages, for this year, for comparison. It should be born in mind that the averages also cover different years.

The weather station is in a suburban back garden in Ochiltree, Dunblane, situated 50 metres to the east of the Dunblane Hydro ridge, 100 metres a.s.l., in a shallow, sheltered valley.

Daily rainfall, maximum and minimum temperatures, barometric pressure, cloud cover and wind direction and speed (Beaufort Scale) are recorded. All except the maximum daily temperatures are recorded at 09.00h. A brief description of the day's weather is also recorded along with notes on exceptional and unusual weather phenomena across the UK and worldwide.

2007 – Highlights

The overall mean temperature was only 0.02°C above the long term average of 8.6°C with night lows 0.03°C below the norm and day highs 0.08°C above it. This was a full degree below the annual mean for the UK of 9.6°C, the latter being the second warmest year on record. In Scotland, it was the third warmest since records began in 1914 and April, with a mean temperature of 10.2°C, was the warmest yet.

There were, as usual, seasonal variations. The mean temperature for the winter period (Dec-Feb) was +0.97°C on the average with the spring (Mar-

May) mean also up by 0.6°C. By contrast, it was the coolest summer since 1998, 1.57°C below the average and 4.55°C below the previous summer! The maximum temperature of 23.8°C was the lowest yearly high to date – some 3.64°C below the mean. The night-time high of 14.2°C was also the lowest annual one yet. Autumn temperatures were just 0.02°C above average.

Total precipitation of 1075.2 mm was slightly below the annual mean of 1101 mm. This however masked some marked seasonal variations. The winter period (Dec–Feb) was the wettest to date, 65 % above the mean. Spring (Mar–May) was only 1 % below normal but it was a wet summer with rainfall 39 % up on the average – the third wettest to date. Autumn was uncharacteristically dry with only 60 % of the normal precipitation – the second driest on record.

January was milder and much wetter than normal with a mean temperature of 3.77°C, 1.2°C above the norm. The average daily temperature was the highest to date at 6.18°C, 1.4°C above the mean and 0.28°C above the previous high. The maximum daily high of 11.7°C was equal to the previous high. 192.1 mm of precipitation made it the wettest January to date, 62.4 % up on the mean and 12 % above the previous high. This made it the seventh wettest month overall in 12 years with the last three months all being in the top seven. Average pressure was below the mean and the ten frosts were three fewer than normal. The garden pond was frozen on five mornings with snow lying on three. It was the warmest January since 1921 for England & Wales.

February was a little milder and drier than the norm with the mean average temperature of 3.75°C up 0.56°C on the mean. The average low was +0.54°C and the average high +0.6°C above the mean. The coldest temperature recorded was -8.1°C (7th) with the warmest being 11.2°C (1st). Precipitation at 81.3 mm was only 76 % of the norm, being measurable on 20 days with a day max. of 19 mm (27th). Air pressure fell to 974 mb (28th), equal to the lowest for the month. There were ten air frosts, two less than the norm with the pond being frozen on seven mornings and snow lying twice at 9 am.

Overall for the UK, the winter quarter of 2006/7 was the equal second warmest after 1868/9 since records began in 1659.

March was slightly warmer and wetter than normal with the mean temperature of +0.32°C and rainfall 20 % above average at 89.9 mm. There were eight frosts – two less than the norm.

April was the warmest to date with the mean temperature of 9.82°C being 2°C above the average and 0.89°C above the previous high in 1997. The average daily high of 14.96°C was 0.93°C higher than the previous best in April 2003. The lowest daytime max of 11°C was also a new high. These warm temperatures also coincided with the second driest April with only 26.5 mm being recorded (21.5 mm in 1995). The average barometric pressure of 1019 mb was equal to the previous high and there was only one air and one ground frost. It was also the warmest April for England & Wales since records began back in 1659 with a mean temperature of 11.1°C – 3.2°C above the average. It was also the sunniest since 1893 and the driest since 1984. UK wide there was only 37 % of normal rainfall with 50 % more sunshine than the norm. In 2006 temperatures didn't breach 20°C anywhere in the UK until the 3rd of May; this year there have been twenty such days before the end of April.

May was cooler & wetter than normal with the mean temperature of 10.13°C being 0.79°C below the average. The average daily high was 0.08°C below that of the previous month! Rainfall, at 90.4 mm, was 25 % above average.

Elsewhere many faired much worse. The late-spring bank holiday weekend was one of the most miserable, with prolonged heavy rain and daytime temperatures the lowest in late May for over half a century. Afternoon temperatures of 5 to 7°C were the lowest in the last week of May since 1948 and play at the Headingly Test Match started on Monday morning (28th) with the temperature reading only 7°C, the lowest in recorded Test cricket history!

June was a little warmer and quite a bit wetter than normal. The mean temperature was +0.11°C with night lows 1.0°C above average and daytime highs 0.8°C cooler. Rainfall was 35 % above the norm with 106.5 mm falling on 20 days. June was the wettest in England & Wales since 1860 and the east coast of Scotland established new lows for sunshine with a total of only 64 hours in Edinburgh – barely a one third of the normal amount.

Daytime maximums remained depressed to the end of the month, the highest being 16.8°C (26th). Heavy downpours badly affected the Midlands & North of England on the 24th / 25th with much flooding in which four people were drowned. 112 mm fell at Fylingdales during this period. The area around Hull and Sheffield was particularly badly affected.

July was the coldest to date with the mean temperature 1.39°C below the average. Daily highs were 1.64°C below the mean with night lows 1.13°C below. It was also the wettest July since 2002 with 96.5 mm – 31 % above the mean, with rainfall recorded on 22 days. Averaged over England & Wales, July was the wettest since 1936 and the coolest since 1993.

The unsettled theme continued until the end of the month depressing temperatures with a maximum of only 13.5°C on the 19th. Such cold air-steams are prone to be very unstable under the summer sun. Hence, hailstones half the size of golf balls fell on Canterbury (15th), when the temperature peaked at 27°C at nearby Herne Bay. Daily maximums were a little better from the 23rd onwards, hovering around the 20°C mark. Torrential downpours occurred across southern Britain on the 20th with several sites in Oxfordshire, Gloucestershire and Worcestershire recording over 100 mm which resulted in much flooding in the river Severn, Avon, Thames and Great Ouse catchments areas. In Gloucestershire more than a third of a million people were left without freshwater. This was the most remarkable July rainstorm since 1969. By contrast, the Western Isles were virtually dry all week.

August was the coldest to date with a mean temperature 0.87°C below the previous low and 1.47°C below the mean. Averaged nationally, it was the coolest since 1993. The average daily low was 1.06°C and the daily high 1.89°C below the mean. The daily high of 13.5°C (18th) was the lowest during August to date and the monthly max day high of 18.4°C was the lowest for August. The monthly precipitation total of 114.9 mm was 50 % above the norm and the third highest August total. Surprisingly, there were only 12 days when recordable amounts of rain fell and only 0.4 mm was recorded during the last 13 days of the month. Most of the rain fell during the first three weekends causing havoc with local cricket fixtures. The 35.4 mm which fell on the 18th was the highest ever daily amount for August.

September was cooler and drier than average with the mean temperature 0.88°C below the norm. The average night low was 1.47°C below the norm – the second lowest to date after September 1995. Precipitation at 57.9 mm was only 66 % of average with almost half of this amount falling on one day. There was measurable rainfall on only 12 days. The air frost on the 27th was the first September frost in 12 years

October was warmer and drier than normal with the mean temperature being +0.62°C above the mean, both the day and night means were above the average. There was only one frost. Rainfall of 63.1 mm was only 46 % of the norm making this the third driest October to date, with measurable rainfall recorded on only 15 days – the lowest number ever. Average pressure of 1020 mb was not only the highest yet for October but also for any month of 2007. The minimum recorded was 1004 mb, the first time that pressure in October hasn't fallen below 1000 mb.

Unsurprisingly then we had to wait until the 24th for the second frost of the winter –1.8°C on the 24th (–5°C in Aboyne, 25th) with dense mist persisting in the Carse of Stirling on both these days although it dispersed quickly in Dunblane to give sunny days .

November was milder and drier than average with the mean temperature 0.58°C above the norm and rainfall, at 80.3 mm, only 73 % of the mean. The min. temperature of 12.2°C during the night of the 1st / 2nd was the warmest November night to date being followed by the warmest November day, 15.2°C (2nd). There were an average number of air frosts with seven.

December's mean temperature of 2.36°C was exactly the same as the long term average with nights 0.33°C below and days 0.36°C above the norm. A succession of Atlantic fronts brought strong winds at the beginning of the month, particularly in the south of Britain with 67 mph recorded at Mumbles (Glamorgan, 1st) and 81 mph (Jersey Airport, 2nd). Pressure rose progressively to the 16th (1035 mb), reaching a UK high of 1040 mb on the 18th). The more settled conditions brought 16 air frosts, the pond was frozen on eight mornings and no snow fell. There was 75.8 mm of rain, 73 % of the norm, with measurable rain fall on 19 days. No more than 0.3 mm fell daily between the 9th and 21st – 13 days.

Table 1. Temperature and rain 2007. N. Bielby Climatological Station Dunblane

	Temp mean maxima	Temp mean minima	Number of Air Frosts	Total rain (mm)	Greatest fall (mm)	Number of days measurable rain
January	6.2 (4.8/6.5)	1.4 (0.4/0.5)	10 (13.5/13)	192 (118/110.7)	21.2 (40.0)	24 (19)
February	6.6 (6.1/6.9)	0.9 (0.4/0.8)	10 (13/11)	81.3 (106/73.2)	19 (31.8)	20 (16)
March	9.0 (8.6/9.1)	1.7 (1.3/1.9)	8 (10/7)	89.9 (74.9/81.4)	22 (44.0)	1 (17)
April	15.0 (12.2/11.8)	4.7 (3.4/3.4)	1 (5/4)	26.5 (60.4/47.5)	10.9 (35.3)	10 (13)
May	14.9 (16.1/15.3)	5.4 (5.8/5.8)	1 (1/1)	90.4 (72.3/56.9)	17.9 (28.3)	20 (14)
June	19.4 (18.2/17.7)	10.0 (8.9/8.4)	0 (<1)	106.5 (79/57.1)	29 (35.8)	20 (13)
July	19.4 (21.0/19.8)	9.6 (10.7/10.6)	0 (0)	96.5 (73.8/62.9)	28 (65.5)	22 (13)
August	18.4 (20.3/19.4)	9.5 (10.5/10.2)	0 (0)	114.9 (76.5/68.1)	35.4 (30.0)	12 (14)
September	15.8 (16.0/16.3)	6.9 (8.4/8.3)	1 (<1)	57.9 (87.6/87.7)	26.5 (44.2)	14 (15)
October	12.7 (11.8/12.9)	5.7 (5.4/5.4)	1 (3/2)	63.1 (137.7/97.9)	14.9 (66.2)	15 (17)
November	7.7 (7.5/9.2)	3.0 (2.1/2.6)	7 (8/8)	80.3 (109.8/98.9)	12.9 (68.3)	24 (17)
December	5.7 (4.4/7.2)	0.0 (0.3/1.1)	13 (13.5/11)	75.8 (103.2/101)	22 (43.8)	19 (18)
Year January-December 2007	13.6 (12.3/13.2)	6.2 (4.9/5.3)	52 (68/58)	979 (1045/943.3)	35.4 (68.3)	216 (186)

The Climatological Normals Bielby/Parkhead are shown in ( )s

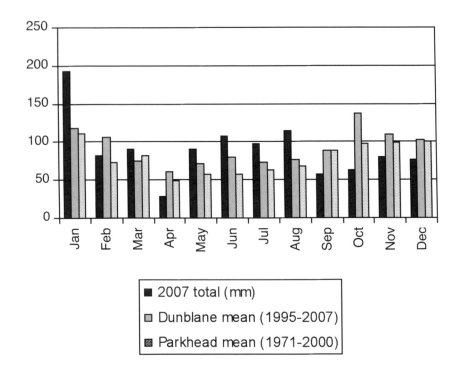

Figure 1. Rainfall 2007.

FORTH AREA BIRD REPORT 2007

A.E. Thiel and C.J. Pendlebury

The present report is the 33rd bird report for the Forth Valley (or Upper Forth) bird recording area. The report was written by Chris Pendlebury (waterfowl, excluding waders, raptors and gamebirds) and Andre Thiel (waders, passerines and escapees) with Cliff Henty contributing the half-monthly summaries to the wader accounts. This autumn Cliff is retiring as SOC Recorder and handing over to Chris Pendlebury who can be contacted by e-mail at chris@upperforthbirds.co.uk or by leaving a message on 07798 711134. However, Cliff will for the present be acting as assistant recorder and, until further notice, as receiver of records or queries from observers. He can be contacted by e-mail at cjh@cliffhenty.plus.com, by mail to 7b Coneyhill Road, Bridge of Allan, FK9 4EL or by phone on 01786 832166.

The main part of the report consists of detailed species accounts presented in a systematic list arranged in the traditional Voous order. This is preceded by a summary of the main bird news from the past year and a Ringing Report, both compiled by Andre Thiel.

ROUND-UP OF THE YEAR

January started with a decent flock of 34 Bramblings at Wester Jawcraigs, Slamannan on 7th. A redhead Smew was at Gart GPs the following day. The Kincardine Bridge area held two Rock Pipits on 16th, while the Forth estuary supported good flocks of 123 Pintail and 10 Scaup on 20th. As in recent years the mild winter encouraged a handful of scarce waders to stay in the Grangemouth area. A Green Sandpiper was on the R. Carron at Carronshore on 15th, up to 3 Greenshanks were recorded at Skinflats during January, dropping to 2 in February and March, and a Ruff overwintered there, being seen between 27th January and 1st March. The Barrow's Goldeneye, which was first seen on 19th Nov 2006 and has now been accepted by the BBRC, continued its stay in the Callander and L Venachar area until 27th April.

The highlight of February was the first Red-breasted Goose for the recording area at Haugh of Blackgrange, Cambus, between 3rd and 11th (and again on 15th April). Observers looking for the bird also spotted 3 Greenland White-fronted Geese there between 5th and 10th. Two immature Golden Eagles were seen over Stuc a' Chroin on 6th when 5 Jack Snipe were at Kinneil. A female Common Scoter was at Kinneil on 25th (as well as on 22nd March). In addition there were three Green Sandpipers: one at the River Avon mouth, Kinneil on 9th, one on the Allan Water at Kinbuck, Dunblane, on 18th and one on the River Forth at Nether Carse on 26th.

March was fairly quiet. A Great Grey Shrike on the western shore of Carron Reservoir on 12th was a good find as was a Spotted Redshank at Kinneil the following day. Two Black-throated Divers at a Trossachs site on 18th were probably birds returning to their breeding grounds. A flock of 8 Gadwall at Cambus Pools on 20th was a good count for our area. Two Waxwings were at Airthrey on 27th and 28th. A Ruff at Skinflats between 31st March and 24th April could have been the overwintering bird or a bird on passage.

April started with a Lesser Scaup at Airthrey on 4th. The first British record of this species was as recently as 1987. There have been over 120 records since, as observers have become increasingly familiar with the identification criteria of this species. This will be the third record for our area, if accepted. Also on 4th two Ptarmigan were seen at Ben More. A Little Ringed Plover at Skinflats on 14th was followed by a pair at Gart GPs on 26th and 27th. Their behaviour seemed to indicate that they were going to breed but the nest site had been bulldozed over by 20th June. A Whimbrel passed at Skinflats on 22nd. Meanwhile numbers of Black-tailed Godwits were building up upstream of the Kincardine Bridge, as they have done so increasingly in recent years. Thirty birds in the Cambus area on 30th March rose to 73 on 11th April, 157 on 21st and 200 on 22nd, while at Devonmouth Pool 61 on 6th rose to 425 on 23rd. These do not seem to be birds moving there from the Grangemouth area, though, at least not in April when numbers there were higher than in 2006. Flocks of 262 at Kinneil and 419 at Skinflats were boosted by an influx of birds of the *islandica* race with 60 of these at Skinflats on 19th and up to 620 on 24th.

Wader spring passage was rather muted this year with a Wood Sandpiper at Skinflats on 12th and 15th May, 4 Whimbrel there on 13th and a Curlew Sandpiper on 20th followed by Sanderlings at Tullibody Inch on 26th and at Kincardine Bridge on 30th. Elsewhere 3 Dotterel on Ben Ledi on 12th was a good find. The same day 3 male Pied Flycatchers were seen at Glen Lochay, while Quail were singing near Gartmorn on 21st and at Blairdrummond Moss on 22nd.

June highlights included a Hobby at Carse of Lecropt on 20th and, as in the preceding two years, a 1st summer Little Gull at Skinflats. Another immature bird was at the Blackdevon Wetlands on 26th. Wader autumn passage started with a Greenshank at Skinflats on 29th.

Wader passage continued at a rather slow pace in July with 2 Whimbrel at Skinflats on 6th and 24th and singles at Kinneil on 10th and 29th and 2 Curlew Sandpipers at Skinflats on 22nd. Elsewhere a sub-adult male Golden Eagle was seen flying over the Braes of Doune on 30th.

August started with the second Hobby of the year flying over Uamh Mhor, Braes of Doune on 2nd. A male Common Scoter was at Kinneil and 2 Curlew Sandpipers at Skinflats, all on the same day. Things picked up during the second week of the month when there were maximum counts of 7 Greenshank at Skinflats on 7th and 16th, 5 Whimbrel and a juvenile Black Tern at Kinneil on 9th, 7 Ruff at Skinflats on 14th rising to up to 13 between 24th and 30th August as well as 14 Snipe there on 25th. Waterside, Braes of Doune, hosted an immature Marsh Harrier on 15th. Two of the highlights of August arrived late in the month. A Little Egret was at Kinneil from 20th to 24th, then at Skinflats on 29th and again at Kinneil on 9th September. This was the 7th record for the recording area, while a Spoonbill at Skinflats on 25th August was the 5th for our area.

September started with the two Fulmars, the only record of the year, at Kinneil on 4th. The only wader highlights of September were up to 8 Ruff at Skinflats between 4th and 9th and a Little Stint there on 9th. Two days later a male Marsh Harrier at Invertrossachs was not a bad sighting. 11 Arctic Skuas and an exceptional 480 Kittiwakes passed Kinneil on 14th. A Manx Shearwater there on 19th was only the 14th record of that species to be seen in our area. The only Great Skua of the year was logged there on 24th. Two Razorbills at Skinflats on 24th, one at Fallin on 28th and 11 at Bo'ness on 29th coincided with the after-effects of strong westerlies during the first part of the month which pushed large numbers of Razorbills into the North Atlantic. An immature White-tailed Eagle from the Tay estuary re-introduction scheme was recorded at Flanders Moss on 27th and was subsequently radio-racked around Argaty in November and December.

October was quieter with the most interesting sightings coming from the Grangemouth area. Two Little Stints at Kinneil on 5th and one at Kincardine Bridge on 13th were the last ones of the year. The monthly Forth estuary count logged a maximum winter count of 58 Scaup on 7th, 45 of which were at Skinflats. On 13th a Black-throated Diver at Kincardine Bridge was the only winter record. An adult Ring-billed Gull at Kinneil was seen on 28th October and subsequently on 4th November and 30th December. This may be the returning bird from 2005 and 2006 and represents the 3rd record for our area, if accepted. Finally an overwintering Ruff was seen repeatedly at Skinflats from 31st to the end of the year.

The start of November saw a good count of Snipe west of Dollar where 15 birds were present on 3rd. At this time of year, there is often an influx of migrants of this species. On 6th there were 3 Greenland White-fronted Geese at Skinflats and an adult Mediterranean Gull at Kinneil. The latter is the 12th occurrence of what is becoming an increasingly regular species in Scotland. The following day a flock of 29 Red Kites were recorded at Argaty. Four days later at Mill of Argaty the only Goshawk of the year was seen, while the only Purple Sandpiper was at Kinneil the same day. A Red-necked Grebe there on 21st was the 14th record of that species. The month finished with an excellent count of 120 Twite at Blackdevon Wetlands on 25th.

December started with the sole Waxwing of the latter part of the year at St. Ninians on 10th. A Great Grey Shrike at Menstrie Glen on 15th was a good find, as were 45 Snow Buntings there the following day. A Green-winged Teal at Kinneil on 21st was only the 4th for our area but this was eclipsed by the undoubted highlight of the year in the form of the first Spotted Sandpiper for our area on the River Avon mouth from 24th till the year end and beyond. The year ended with 80 Ravens at their traditional roost of Doune Lodge on 30th.

RECORD SUBMISSION AND REPORT FORMAT

Annual Bird Reports depend largely on contributions from the local birdwatching community. Due to the ever growing (and welcome) volume of data that are submitted, some data that may be of relevance in one year may not be so in another year. This should not discourage contributors from submitting data that they feel are of relevance to their local area, as it will only become obvious whether a particular record should be included or not once the entire dataset is available. Several observers send in a list largely or entirely for their home locality. Much of this information is not appropriate for inclusion in these annual reports but it is valuable to have on record (e.g. for conservation action). These are kept in a special file. At the moment there are fifteen such lists referring to the whole district from Falkirk to Killin. Several contributors send in data, often of common species, from repeated transect visits to the same locality, e.g. Airthrey; King's Park, Stirling; Cobleland, Aberfoyle. This has become more common since the advent of the BTO's Birdtrack on-line project. Such data reflect birds per walked route rather than flock sizes. These data are especially useful, if collected repeatedly and using the same effort between years, as it allows valid comparison between seasons and years to be made.

To facilitate the preparation of the report, contributors are strongly encouraged to submit their data as soon as possible after the end of the year. Electronic files are much the preferred format, as it greatly speeds up cross-checking and summarising of data. A standard spreadsheet is available from Chris Pendlebury. Special thanks are due to those contributors who are now submitting their data in this format.

Following on from the past years, an increasing number of records are submitted with 6-figure grid references. This is strongly encouraged, as it enormously speeds up cross-checks and is a valuable resource for conservation action. Also more contributors add the name of the nearest village which, too, is very much appreciated.

The sparse information available about common breeding species is improved by data from the Breeding Birds Survey (BBS). For less common species data can sometimes be summarised in terms of the numbers of pairs or apparently occupied territories for particular locations. The organisers for both the estuary and the inland waters parts of the national wildfowl counts (WeBS) have also made available the results from these for this report. Where appropriate, these are included in the species accounts.

For many species the records sent in are very unrepresentative of their general distribution. This applies particularly to very common species or to those that are secretive or breed in inaccessible locations. The status of species is detailed in a check list, published in the *Forth Naturalist and Historian*, Vol 15. Additional information along with guidelines for the submission of records can be obtained from N. Bielby, 56 Ochiltree, Dunblane, FK15 0DF (tel. 01786 823830, e-mail: n.bielby@sky.com). In addition there is a coded summary of general distribution after the species name. This often apparently contradicts the detailed records that are published for the year. The codes are thus:

B - Breeding status: widespread (present in more than five 10 km squares)
b   "   " :   local, scarce (present in fewer than five 10 km squares)
W - Winter status: widespread or often in groups of more than ten
w -   "   " :   local, scarce (usually fewer than ten in a group)
P :   Passage (used when species is usually absent in winter;
                        P or p used for widespread or local as in winter status)
S or s :   Summer visitor (used for species present in summer but
                        which do not normally breed; S or s used for
                        widespread or local as in winter status).

Thus BW would be appropriate for Robin, B for Swallow, p for Ruff and SW for Cormorant. No status letter is used if a species occurs less than every other year.

The SOC has in the past pressed for a more systematic vetting of records of species that are unusual locally. Our area has an informal panel of five members: C. Henty, C. Pendlebury, D. Orr-Ewing, M.V. Bell, and A. McIver. The panel has produced a list of species that are scarce locally and where the records need to be supported by either a full description or sufficient evidence to remove any reasonable doubt. The list is available from Chris Pendlebury. Any species which is a vagrant to the area and some of those which are asterisked (*) in this report will fall in this category. At the discretion of the panel a description may also be required for more common species. The judging of Scottish or national rarities continues as before and descriptions need to be submitted to the relevant committees. The first twenty occurrences of a species in our recording area are noted.

The British Ornithologists' Union (BOU) has appealed in the past for introduced/escaped species to be recorded locally. As the published information on these species is not necessarily complete, self-sustaining populations of such species may exist which are not known about or adequately recorded. The BOU therefore encourages observers to record and monitor all naturalised species (particularly but not exclusively breeding records and interactions with native species) and escaped species seen in the wild to assist it to make future recommendations for category C status, if a self-sustaining naturalised population is established.

The following abbreviations have been used in the report: Ad(s) - adult(s), AoT - apparently occupied territory, b/lkm - birds per linear kilometre, Br - bridge, BoA - Bridge of Allan, BoD - Braes of Doune, ca - circa, c/n - clutch of n eggs, conf. - confluence, BBS - Breeding Bird Survey, CP - Country Park, E - east, Est - estuary, Fm - farm, F - Female, G - Glen, GP - gravel pit, Imm - immature, incl - including, Juv - juvenile, L - Loch, N - north, NR - Nature Reserve, nr - near, M - Male, Max - maximum, ON - on nest; pr - pair; Res - Reservoir, R - river, Rd - road, S - south, SP - summer plumage, W - west, WeBS - Wetland Bird Survey, Y - young, , > flying/flew.

The area covered by the report comprises the council areas of Falkirk and Clackmannan together with Stirling, excluding Loch Lomondside and other parts of the Clyde drainage basin. Please note that we do not include the Endrick Water, i.e. Fintry and Balfron.

CONTRIBUTORS

This report has been compiled from records submitted by the contributors listed below. Where initials are given, the contributors are listed in the species entries.

M. Alexander, D. Anderson (DA), M. Anderson, P. Ashworth (PMA), A. Ayre (AA), B. Barker (BB), Bean Goose Action Group (BGAG), G. Boath, M. Bell (MVB), N. Bielby (NB), Birdguides (BRG), A. Blair (AB), R.A. Broad (RAB), K. Broomfield (KB), D. M. Bryant (DMB), A. Bryson, J. Calladine (JRC), D. Cameron (DJC), G. Cannon, I. Carmichael, A. Carrington-Cotton (ACC), P. Carter, Central Scotland Black Grouse and Capercaillie Group (CSBGCG), R. Chapman, D. and A. Christie (DAC), C. Clark, S.R. Cook, M. Cooper, T. Craig, R. Daly, R. Dalziel (RDZ), Ben Darvill (BD), R. and H. Dawson (RHD), A. Derks (AD), J. Dewberry, R. Downie, K. Duffy (KD), R. Eaves (RE), D. Egerton, T. Findlay (TF), Forestry Commission Scotland (FCS), Forthbirding, C. Fraser, G. Fraser, J. Fulton (JF), G. Garner (GG), T. Goater, A. Gowans, J. Grainger, S. Green, A. Hannah, W. D. Harris, I. Hartley (IH), C. Henty (CJH), D. Hodgson, K. Hoey (KH), D Holland, J. Holland (JPH), Liz Humphries (EMH), P. D. Hunt, L. Johnson, D. Kerr (DK), J. Kaye, R. Knight, A. Lauder, D. Lang, P. Lee, G. and E. Leisk (GEL), P. Lubbers (PAL), C. Lyddon (CL), R. Mair, C. Mallett (CJM), K. S. Mann, D. Matthews, R. McBeath, L. McBrien (LMB), M. McGinty (MMcG), R. McKee, K. Maclean (KMcl), G. Mcphail, P. McSorley (PMS), A. Masterman (AM), N. Melsom (NM), S. Milligan, C. Moore, D. Morrison (DM), F. Murray (FAM), D. Orr-Ewing (DOE), I.B. Osborn, G. Owens (GO), J. and E. Payne, C.J. Pendlebury (CJP), D. Pickett, Keith Pilkington, S. Rae, D. Redwood, C. Renwick (CR), S. Renwick (SRE), G. Richards (GR), R. Ridley (RR), E. Rimmer, M. Roberts, J. Robertson (JGR), D. Robertson, A.C. Rogers (ACR), N. Rossiter, David Rugg, A. Samson, M. Scott, R. and S. Sexton, R. Shand (RS), J. Shanks (JS), A. Simpkins, H. Simpson, G. Skipper, K. Smith, A. Smith, E. Smy (ES), C. Spray, M. Stephen, N. & M. Suess, P. Sutton, Stirling District Ranger Service, Rob Swift (RSW), D. Taylor, P. Taylor, A. Thiel (AET), M. Thoroe (MT), D. Thorogood (DT), J. Towill (JT), M. Towill, L. Turner, M. Trubridge, C. Twist (CT), N. Trout, C. Walker, A.E. Watterson, T. Wells, C. Wernham, J.S. Wilson, R. Wilson, L. Winskill, M. Wotherspoon (MWO), H. Young.

WeBS estuary counts are made available by M. Bell. Thanks are also due to J. Nadin for the kind permission to use his photo of the Spotted Sandpiper. Apologies to anybody who has been inadvertently missed out of the above list.

RINGING REPORT

This is the fourth ringing report. The following section lists all ringed birds seen in the recording area during the year. Contributors are encouraged to report colour-ringed wildfowl to the relevant organisers and/or the BTO and not to assume that somebody else has already done so, as all movements are of interest to the ringers and add to our understanding of bird ecology and migration patterns. Thanks are due to Allan and Lyndesay Brown, Les Hatton and Shirley Millar (Tay Ringing Group-TRG) and Bob Swann for making available data on movements of birds seen in the recording area.

Fourteen recoveries (excluding multiple sightings of the same bird) were made in 2007. Most are, not surprisingly, of Pink-footed Geese (4), Greylag Geese (3) and Mute Swan (1). Others related to Black-tailed Godwit (2), Pied Wagtail, Sedge Warbler, Great Tit and Chaffinch. The total number of species for which ringing information is now available for our area (since 2004) currently stands at 22 species.

Allan and Lyndesay Brown, who are ringing Mute Swans in Fife and the Lothians, are particularly keen to learn if any of the birds ringed by them (green or white Darvic rings) breed outside their study area.

Recoveries are listed in Voous order, as for the systematic list, under the headings shown below. Where an asterisk appears behind a ring number, further details of sightings are given in previous ringing reports.

Ring number	Date ringed	Location ringed	Date seen	Location in recording area (codes as in main list)	Recorder

followed by the location(s) where the bird was seen in between

•PINK-FOOTED GOOSE

| Grey neck ISX | 28 Jul 2000 | Nautalda, Thjorsarver, Arness, ICELAND | 17 Feb 2007 | Netherton, Thornhill (S) | JT |

This bird was re-sighted the same year in NW England where it was seen at Martin Mere (Lancashire) in Oct, Kirkby (Merseyside) in Nov and Pilling (Lancashire) in Dec. The following year it stopped over at Loch of Strathbeg in Oct 2001 before heading back to Martin Mere (Lancashire) two weeks later and then Fylde (Lancashire) in Dec 2001. A similar story in 2002 when it was re-sighted at Loch Meikle (Aberdeenshire) in Oct. There were no further re-sightings until the Thornhill record.

| Grey neck IZH | 29 Jul 2000 | Oddkelsalda, Thjorsarver, Arness, ICELAND | 17 Feb 2007 | Netherton, Thornhill (S) | JT |

Although showing similarities to the above bird (both were ringed as adult males in Iceland), this bird seems to have been more faithful to Central Scotland. It was first re-sighted near Perth (Perth and Kinross) in Oct 2000, then near Flanders Moss and Blairdrummond Moss the next month where it was again seen in April 2001. By Nov 2001 it was present near Auchterarder (Perth & Kinross), then at North Mid Frew Farm, Stirling in Jan 2001, Culmore Farm, Stirling in Mar 2001. There were no further sightings until the Thornhill record.

| Grey neck PJI | 20 Nov 2005 | Loch of Lintrathen (Angus) | 17 Mar 2007 | Gogar, Menstrie (S) | AET |

No sightings in between.

| Grey neck TUI | 22 Oct 2006 | Loch of Lintrathen (Angus) | 26 Oct 2007 | Tullygarth, Alloa (C) | AET |

First re-sighted at Munlochy (Ross & Cromarty) in April 2007.

•GREYLAG GOOSE

Grey neck BZV*	28 Jul 1997	Masvatn, S-Ping	14 Jan 2007	Kersiepow	AET
		ICELAND	19 Jan 2007	Kersiepow	
			21 Jan 2007	East Gogar	
				(C, S)	

Having spent most winter visits between 1998 and 2003 in Fife, this bird was first recorded in Clackmannanshire in Feb 2004. It has since been recorded repeatedly in Clackmannanshire with the occasional foray back into Fife. The above sightings refer to its fourth consecutive winter appearance in our area.

Grey neck HCA*	24 Feb 2000	Loch Eye	14 Jan 2007	Kersiepow	AET
		(Easter Ross)	21 Jan 2007	Kersiepow	
			21 Jan 2007	Gogar	
			17 Mar 2007	Gogar	
				(C, S)	

Following sightings nr. Montrose (Angus) and in Iceland in 2001, this bird was seen at Drymen, Stirlingshire, in Jan 2003. It has since been a regular visitor to Clackmannanshire, notably Sheardale nr Dollar (Mar 2003, Feb 2004) and the area between Alva and Tillicoultry (Oct 2004 to Jan 2005), before relocating to the Cambus-Gogar area in Jan and Mar 2005 and in 2006. In 2007 It returned to our area for its 5th consecutive winter.

Red neck BKL	13 Nov 2004	Loch Eye (Easter Ross)	14 Jan 2007	Kersiepow	AET
			19 Jan 2007	Kersiepow	
			21 Jan 2007	Kersiepow	
			21 Jan 2007	Gogar	
				(C, S)	

In Nov 2005 at Kinbeachie, then Udale Bay (both Cromarty Firth) Dec 2005. After its stay in Clackmannanshire in Feb and Mar 2006, the bird was seen at Akurbrekka, Hrutafjordur, **Iceland** on 28 Sep 2006. It returned to Clackmannanshire for its second consecutive winter.

•MUTE SWAN

Green IFT*	21 Aug 2004	Stenton Pond, Glenrothes	19 Mar 2007	Gartmorn Dam	AET
		(Fife)		(C)	

Last seen at Stenton Pond on 7 Feb 2005, then at the Boll, Alva in Feb, Mar and Apr 2006 and again there in Jan and Feb 2007.

•BLACK-TAILED GODWIT

Colour-ringed	27 Jun 2005	Flaga, Arnessysla,	23 to 31 Aug 2006	Kinneil	DT
		SOUTH ICELAND		(C)	

Also seen 14 Aug 2005 Olonne-sur-Mer, Vendée, WESTERN FRANCE

Colour-ringed	5 Jul 2004	Langhus, Fljot	23 to 31 Aug 2006	Kinneil	DT
		NORTH ICELAND		(C)	

Also seen 18-21 Apr 2006 Kralingerploder, Midden-Delfland, Zuid Holland, WEST NETHERLANDS and 24 Apr 2006 Leidschendam, Zuid Holland, WEST NETHERLANDS

•PIED WAGTAIL

T120944	3 Jun 2005	Letter, Loch Katrine (S)	16 Nov 2006	Tarleton,	TRG
				nr. Preston (Lancashire)	

Found dead at a distance of 306 km SSE after 166 days.

•SEDGE WARBLER

T387550	21 May 2005	Blackgrange (C)	9 Aug 2005	Titchfield Haven,	TRG
				Fareham (Hampshire)	

Caught and released at a distance of 614 km SSE after 80 days.

•GREAT TIT

TC44596	11 Jun 2005	Brenachoile NW, Loch Katrine (S)	1 Jan 2006	Tarbert, Cnoc, Loch Lomond (Argyll & Bute)	TRG

Caught and released at a distance of 15 km WSW after 204 days.

•CHAFFINCH

R273088	5 Apr 2003	Allt Beithe, Strathyre (S)	14 Apr 2006	Strathyre (S)	TRG

Remarkably this bird was found dead at the same locality as it was ringed after 3 years and 9 days.

SYSTEMATIC LIST

Codes - S, F and C indicate records from Stirling, Falkirk and Clackmannanshire "Districts".

RED-THROATED DIVER *Gavia stellata* (b, w)

F   Singles Kinneil 20 Jan and 18 Feb (JRC). 2 Kinneil 19 Sep (DT). 2 off Skinflats 24 Sep (CJP, BD). 1 Bo'ness 29 Sep (DT). Singles Kinneil 5 and 28 Oct (DT). 1 Skinflats 25 Oct (MVB). 1 Kinneil 21 Dec (GO).

Addition from 2006: 7 Kinneil 26 Nov (DT).

BLACK-THROATED DIVER *Gavia arctica* (b, w)

F   1 Kincardine Br 13 Oct (CJP, BD).

S   2 undisclosed sites in the Trossachs: 2 birds on 18 Mar (RR); 1 pr 5 May (DAC).

LITTLE GREBE *Tachybaptus ruficollis* (B, w)

      Inland WeBS counts: 53 in Jan, 59 in Feb, 32 in Mar, 46 in Sep, 87 in Oct, 76 in Nov, 79 in Dec

F   Max: 6 Drumbowie Res 1 Oct; 11 Little Denny Res 1 Oct; 5 Black Loch 1 Oct; 5 Kinneil 31 Dec.

C   Breeding: 1 pr and 2 Y Lawmuir Pond, Dollar 26 May. Site max: 6 R Devon, Alva-Menstrie 13 Feb; 8 Gartmorn Dam 24 Aug; 6 Silverhills Pond, Kersiepow 19 Sep and 20 Oct; 3 Blackdevon Wetlands 21 Sep.

S   Breeding: 1 pr David Marshall Lodge Pond 8 Mar; 1 pr Doune Ponds 20 Mar; 2 prs L Ard 12 May; 1 pr Upper Lanrick 27 May; 2 prs Cambusmore. Site max: 24 Cambusmore 22 Sep; 16 L Dochart 22 Nov; 9 L Voil 3 Feb; 8 Carron Valley Res 8 Oct; 7 Airthrey Loch 12 Mar; 7 Blair Drummond 4 Oct.

GREAT CRESTED GREBE *Podiceps cristatus* (b, W)

      Inland WeBS counts: 6 in Jan, 32 in Feb, 36 in Mar, 26 in Sep, 22 in Oct, 5 in Nov, 6 in Dec.

      Forth Est (WeBS) Jan to Mar max: 8 on 20 Jan; Sep to Dec max: 49 on 7 Oct.

F   Site max: 44 Kinneil 5 Oct.

C   Site max: 6 Gartmorn Dam 31 Mar.

S   Breeding: 2 prs Cambusmore fledged 1 Y; pr Blair Drummond 6 Apr; pr L. Rusky 17 Apr; ad and imm Carron Valley Res Sep and Oct. Max: 21 Lake of Menteith 9 Feb; 7 Carron Valley Res 12 Mar.

SLAVONIAN GREBE *Podiceps auritus*

S   1 L Coulter 5 Dec (NB).

RED-NECKED GREBE *Podiceps grisegena*

F   1 Kinneil 21 Nov (DMB). This is the 14th record for the recording area.

FULMAR *Fulmarus glacialis*

F   2 Kinneil 4 Sep (GO).

Addition from 2006: 2 Kinneil 16 Sep (DT).

MANX SHEARWATER *Puffinus puffinus*

S   1 Kinneil 19 Sep flew low over mudflats before flying E (DT). This is the 14th record for our area since modern recording began in 1974.

GANNET *Morus bassanus* (p)
F   Juv Kinneil 14 Sep (MVB); 15 juvs there 19 Sep (DT); 18 juvs Skinflats 21 Sep (GO); 4 > Carron 22 Sep (AB); 32 Skinflats 23 Sep (GG), 45 there 24 Sep (CJP, BD); juv Bo'ness 29 Sep (DT); 6 juvs Kinneil 5 Oct (DT); juv Skinflats 7 Oct (MVB); 3 juvs Kinneil 28 Oct (DT).
S   5 juvs > W at Stirling 19 Sep. 3 > N at Dunblane 20 Sep (KD). 6 Doune 24 Sep (GG). 30 > W at Flanders Moss 28 Sep (DAP). 7 > W at Plean 28 Sep (RS).

CORMORANT *Phalacrocorax carbo* (S, W)
      Inland WeBS counts: 82 in Jan, 80 in Feb, 66 in Mar, 44 in Sep, 64 in Oct, 96 in Nov, 81 in Dec.
F   38 Alloa 25 Mar.
C   11 Blackgrange 23 Oct.
S   Max: 19 N Third Res 13 Nov; 15 Lake of Menteith 28 Sep; 11 Carron Valley Res 10 Nov; 11 Airthrey 3 Dec.

*LITTLE EGRET *Egretta garzetta* (S, W)
F   1 Kinneil 20-24 Aug, also at Skinflats 29 Aug and at Kinneil again 9 Sep (DMB, RS, GO, DT). This is the 7th record for our area since modern recording began in 1974, reflecting the recent spread of this species in Britain. The first bird was recorded in 2002.

GREY HERON *Ardea cinerea* (B, W)
      Inland WeBS counts: 108 in Jan, 90 in Feb, 60 in Mar, 65 in Sep, 116 in Oct, 90 in Nov, 93 in Dec.
      BBS: recorded at 0.1 b/1km, similar to annual mean.
F   Max: 40 Skinflats 15 Sep; 15 Powfoulis 10 Jul.
C   Max: 11 Alloa 22 Jan.
S   Max: 19 Teith / Forth conf 21 Jan; 13 Alloa, R Forth 15 Dec.

*SPOONBILL *Platalea leucorodia*
F   1 Skinflats 25 Aug (GG). This is the 5th record of this species since modern recording began and the 4th since 2000. Like Little Egret, this species is also expanding its range in Britain.

MUTE SWAN *Cygnus olor* (B, W)
      Inland WeBS counts: 195 in Jan, 208 in Feb, 179 in Mar, 132 in Sep, 157 in Oct, 178 in Nov, 195 in Dec.
F   13 Skinflats 24 Apr.
C   Breeding: pr Blackdevon Wetlands 27 Apr; pr with 7 Y Naemoor Pond 12 Jun; pr with 7 Y R Devon, Menstrie Jun to Aug. Max: 37 Gartmorn 26 Nov; 28 The Boll, Alva 19 Jan; 24 Cambus Village Pool 13 Apr.
S   Breeding: pr and 5 Y Cambusmore 17 Jun, 3 juvs still 15 Aug; pr Doune Lodge, BoD. Max: 25 Airthrey Loch 29 Oct; 26 R Forth, Stirling 18 Feb; 13 Lake of Menteith 8 Mar.

WHOOPER SWAN *Cygnus cygnus* (W)
      Inland WeBS counts: 58 in Jan, 90 in Feb, 29 in Mar, 3 in Sep, 11 in Oct, 31 in Nov and Dec.
F   Winter/spring: 12 ads Bonnybridge 3 Mar; 9 > W off Blackness Castle 27 Mar. Autumn/winter: 5 Skinflats 4 to 11 Nov, 4 still there 23 Nov; 13 > W at Carron 6 Nov; 3 St. Helen's Loch, Bonnybridge 3 Dec.
C   Winter/spring: 2 > W at Alva 2 Apr; 1 R Forth, Cambus 4 Apr; 37 > W at Alva 11 Apr. Autumn/winter: 7 Blackgrange 23 Oct; 1 > at E Cambus 2 Nov; 4 > at Clackmannan 25 Nov; 2 Gartmorn Dam 26 Nov.
S   Winter/spring: 14 > SW at Dunblane 6 Jan; 10 ads > E at Lecropt Carse 14 Jan; 17 Nether Carse, Forth 29 Jan; 10 L Coulter 6 Feb; 25 L Dochart 16 Feb; 12 Carron Valley Res 18 Feb; 13 L Mahaick 19 Mar. Autumn/winter: 1 Lake of Menteith 28

Sep; 26 > W at Lecropt Carse 2 Dec; 18 L Dochart 15 Dec; 10 Carron Valley Res 15 Dec.

BEAN GOOSE *Anser fabalis* (W)
F   Slamannan plateau: 160 on 12 Feb; last spring record of 40 on 27 Feb; 81 on 28 Sep were the first autumn birds with 271 on 21 Oct and 300 (2007 max.) on 22 Nov (BGAG).

PINK-FOOTED GOOSE *Anser brachyrhynchus* (W)
Last spring record: 1 G Finglas 27 May. First autumn return: 6 > W at Kinneil 14 Sep (DT).
F   Winter/spring: 3380 Airth 23 Feb; 740 Skinflats 1 Mar. Autumn/winter: 2000 Skinflats 31 Oct.
C   Winter/spring: 2000+ Alloa Inch 22 Jan and 3 Mar; 3000 Haugh of Blackgrange 5 Feb, 1500 there 15 Apr; 1810 Kennetpans 18 Feb. Autumn/winter: 325 Alloa 26 Oct; 550 Alva 29 Dec.
S   Winter/spring: 2000 Thornhill 17 Feb; 1500 Flanders Moss 20 Feb; 1720 Ashfield 12 Mar. Autumn/winter: 1815 > NE at Ashfield 28 Sep; 1500 > W at Flanders Moss towards Lake of Menteith 4 Nov; 1750+ Lecropt Carse 2 Dec.

WHITE-FRONTED GOOSE *Anser albifrons* (w)
F   3 birds of the Greenland race at Skinflats 6 Nov (AB).
C   3 birds of the Greenland race at Haugh of Blackgrange 5-6 Feb, with 2 there till 10 Feb (RS).

GREYLAG GOOSE *Anser anser* (b, W)
F   Winter/spring: 310 Airth 18 Feb. Summer (feral): 90 Skinflats 27 Jul. Autumn/winter: 200 Skinflats 12 Sept; 130 Bonnybridge 9 Dec.
C   Winter/spring: 432 Alva 19 Jan; 520 Cambus Pools 21 Jan; 320 Tullibody Inch 4 Feb. Autumn/winter: 233 Alva floods 10 Dec.
S   Winter/spring: 216 Ashfield 12 Mar; 300 Thornhill Carse 21 Mar. Summer (feral): 26 Cambusmore 5 Jun. Autumn/winter: 600 L. Coulter 23 Oct; 320 Gogar 7 Dec.

CANADA GOOSE *Branta canadensis* (b, W)
Inland WeBS counts: 474 in Jan, 379 in Feb, 194 in Mar, 150 in Sep, 502 in Oct, 310 in Nov, 334 in Dec.
F   Site max: 201 St. Helen's Loch, Bonnybridge 16 Jan, 147 there 3 Dec; 31 Airth 19 Sep.
C   Site max: 70 Alloa Inch 6 Sep; 15 Blackdevon Marshes 20 Sep.
S   Breeding: pr and 5 Y Cambusmore, 4 Y still 5 June. 13 May. Site max: 101 Lake of Menteith 21 Jan; 176 L Venachar 1 Feb; 257 G Finglas Res in July; 318 L Coulter 1 Oct; 119 Killin 15 Dec.

BARNACLE GOOSE *Branta leucopsis* (w)
F   1 St. Helen's Loch, Bonnybridge 16 Jan (NB); 50 > SW at Bo'ness 27 Sep (RS); 55 Skinflats 30 Sep (RS); 34 > W at Skinflats 5 Oct (RS); 1 Skinflats 6 Oct (GG).
C   1 Haugh of Blackgrange 8 to 11 Feb (DT, NB).
S   7 Ashfield 12 Mar (MVB); 3 Lecropt Carse 2 Dec (DT); 1 Ledcharrie, G Dochart 15 Dec (NB).
Addition from 2006: 6 Lecropt Carse 9 Dec (DT).

*RED-BREASTED GOOSE *Branta ruficollis* (w)
C   1 Haugh of Blackgrange 3 to 11 Feb, and again 15 Apr (RHD *et al*). This is the first record for the Upper Forth area and has been accepted by BBRC.

SHELDUCK *Tadorna tadorna* (b, W)
Forth Est (WeBS) Jan to Mar max: 767 on 17 Mar; Sep to Dec max: 2621 on 15 Sep.
F   Breeding: 3 prs with broods of 6, 8, and 9 Y Avon Mouth, Kinneil 25 Jun, broods of 3 and 6 still 21 Jul. Moult flock: 2220 Kinneil 28 Jul; peaking at 3929 at Kinneil and 571 at Skinflats on 20 Aug.

C   Breeding: 2 prs Blackdevon Wetlands 27 Apr; 4 prs Cambus Village Pool and 1 pr Devonmouth Pool 28 Apr. Site max: 64 Blackdevon Wetlands 1 May.

S   2 Lecropt Carse 18 May.

WIGEON *Anas penelope* (b, W)

Inland WeBS counts: 681 in Jan, 822 in Feb, 461 in Mar, 67 in Sep, 303 in Oct, 520 in Nov, 741 in Dec.

Forth Est (WeBS) Jan to Mar max: 1020 on 18 Feb; Sep to Dec max: 459 on 19 Dec.

F   Winter/spring site max: 241 Skinflats 20 Jan; 50 Dunmore 11 Feb. Summer: pr Skinflats throughout. Autumn/winter site max: 50 Kinneil 29 Sep.

C   Winter/spring site max: 130 Dunmore, R Forth 11 Feb; 168 Blackdevon Wetlands 13 Feb; Summer: pr Blackdevon Wetlands 4 May. Autumn/winter site max: 52 Kersiepow 7 Dec.

S   Winter/spring site max: 187 Cambusmore 1 Feb; 100 E Frew 26 Feb. Summer: 2 prs Cambusmore 26 Apr, 1 pr there 5 June. Winter/spring site max.: 114 L Coulter 2 Nov; 123 Killin 15 Dec.

Addition from 2006 breeding record: F and Y Gart GP 26 Jun.

GADWALL *Anas strepera* (s, w)

F   1 Skinflats 31 Mar (GO). 2 Kinneil 15 Dec, also on 22-24 Dec (GO, RS, AB).

C   Cambus Pools: 2 on 18 Mar; 8 on 20 Mar; up to 7 (3 prs) in Apr; 1-2 prs in May (RLG, DMB, NB, CJH). 1 pr Blackdevon Wetlands 25 Apr and 4 May (CJH).

S   Pr Culnagreine L 1 Feb (NB). 1 L Voil 18 Nov (NM).

TEAL *Anas crecca* (b, W)

Inland WeBS counts: 1101 in Jan, 988 in Feb, 685 in Mar, 143 in Sep, 497 in Oct, 871 in Nov, 1084 in Dec.

Forth Est (WeBS) Jan to Mar max: 1146 on 20 Jan; Sep to Dec max.: 775 on 7 Oct.

F   Winter/spring site max: 287 Skinflats 18 Feb. Summer: 1 Skinflats 12 May. Autumn/winter site max: 88 A905-Carronhouse, R Forth 17 Feb and 64 Carronhouse-Carronbridge, R Forth 19 Feb; 400 Kinneil 23 Dec.

C   Winter/spring site max: 215 Dollar-Tillicoultry 23 Jan; 95 Cambus Pools 9 Apr. Autumn/winter site max.: 99 Blackdevon Wetlands 5 Dec; 106 Dollar - Tillicoultry 19 Dec.

S   Winter/spring site max: 170 Fallin 21 Jan; 79 L Voil 3 Feb; 86 L Mahaick 18 Feb. Summer: F and 6 Y Flanders Moss 26 Jun, still 9 Aug. Autumn/winter site max: 85 Carron Valley Res 10 Nov; 118 Fallin 10 Dec.

*GREEN-WINGED TEAL *Anas carolinensis*

F   M Kinneil 21 Dec to year-end (GO *et al.*). This is the 4th record for the area since modern recording began in 1974.

MALLARD *Anas platyrhynchos* (B, W)

Inland WeBS counts: 2239 in Jan, 2071 in Feb, 1080 in Mar, 1178 in Sep, 2129 in Oct, 2339 in Nov, 2567 in Dec.

Forth Est (WeBS) Jan to Mar max: 243 on 20 Jan; Sep to Dec max: 294 on 7 Oct.

BBS: recorded at 0.3 b/1km, lower than the annual mean.

F   60 at Kinneil 28 Jul.

C   Breeding: F and 12 Y Blackdevon Wetlands 25 Apr, 7 Y still 16 May; F and 6 Y Gartmorn Dam 26 Apr; 2 broods of 15 Y and 9 Y Cambus Village Pool 10 May.

S   Summer: F and 6 Y Polmaise Lagoons. Site max:151 Airthrey Loch 22 Oct; 52 Nether Carse 26 Nov.

PINTAIL *Anas acuta* (W)

Forth Est (WeBS) Jan to Mar max: 123 on 20 Jan; Sep to Dec max: 37 on 9 Dec.

F   Majority of above at Skinflats and Kinneil. Site max: 87 at Skinflats 20 Jan; 50 at Kinneil 5 Jan.

S   1 Callander 8 Apr. 2 L Tay 29 Apr.

SHOVELER *Anas clypeata* (p)
F   Skinflats: pr on 18 Jun; 2 F on 26 Aug; 4 on 30 Aug (GO, AB).
C   2 M and F Blackdevon Wetlands 30 Mar; 2 prs on 25 Apr, 2 pr. and 1 M on 1 May;
     2 M on 4 May; 1 M on 31 May; 2 on 16 Oct; 1 on 25 Nov; 1 M on 5 Dec (CJH,
     DMB). 3 Tullibody Inch 3 Mar and 15 Apr (DMB). 2 M and F Cambus Village
     Pool 9 Apr; 1 M on 11 Apr and 23 May; 1 F on 19 Sep (NB).
S   1 M Cambusmore 26 Apr (DT). 2 Doune Lodge, BoD 28 Apr (DOE).
POCHARD *Aythya ferina* (W)
     Inland WeBS counts: 8 in Jan, 3 in Feb, 17 in Mar, 2 in Sep, 7 in Oct, 69 in Nov,
     47 in Dec.
F   2 Kinneil 5 Sep; 1 on 14 Sep; 7 on 19 Sep; 2 M on 5 Oct. F Skinflats 14 Oct.
C   1 Blackgrange 21 Jan. 6 Gartmorn Dam 7 Aug.
S   16 Cambusmore 6 Mar. 22 Carron Valley Res 10 Nov. 27 Lake of Menteith 29
     Nov and 16 Dec.
Addition from 2006: 38 Cambusmore 5 Nov.
TUFTED DUCK *Aythya fuligula* (B, W)
     Inland WeBS counts: 371 in Jan, 378 in Feb, 225 in Mar, 245 in Sep, 568 in Oct,
     531 in Nov, 327 in Dec.
F   Site max: 30 Black Loch, Limerigg 6 Feb; 30 St Helen's Loch, Bonnybridge 2 Nov.
C   Site max: 141 Gartmorn Dam 20 Jan; 36 Silverhills Pond, Kersiepow 19 Jan; 7
     Alva 11 May.
S   Breeding: 2 broods Cambusmore 8 Jul, 1 Y still 15 Aug. Site max: 77 Lake of
     Menteith 30 Oct; 64 Vale of Cousty 20 Mar; 59 L Coulter 1 Oct; 49 Airthrey Loch
     31 Jan; 37 L Walton 18 Feb; 37 N Third Res 13 Nov.
SCAUP *Aythya marina* (s, w)
     Forth Est (WeBS) Jan to Mar max: 10 on 20 Jan; Sep to Dec max: 58 on 7 Oct.
F   Kinneil: up to 6 in Jan; F on 7 Mar; F on 6-24 April; M on 12 Apr; 3 on 6 Aug
     and 29 Sep; max of 9 (4 M and 5 F) in Oct on 19th; max of 9 in Nov on 25th;
     max of 7 in Dec (DAC, DMB, GO *et al.*). Skinflats: F on 30 Sep; 45 on 7 Oct, 4 F
     on 19th and 2 F on 29th (MVB, AB, DAC). F Dunmore 14 Oct (AB). 1 Drumbowie
     30 Dec (JS).
S   M Airthrey L from previous year to 18 May (CJP, ACC). 1 Coustry Pond 4 Oct
     (NB). 1 Polmaise Lagoons 23 Nov (DAC).
*LESSER SCAUP *Aythya affinis*
S   M Airthrey Loch 4 Apr (IH). This bird was photographed and will be the third
     record for area if accepted by BBRC.
EIDER *Somateria mollissima* (w, s)
     Forth Est (WeBS) Jan to Mar max: 32 on 8 Feb; Sep to Dec max: 15 on 15 Sep.
F   Kinneil: imm M on 25 Feb; 8 on 22 Mar; imm. M on 24 Apr; F and 5 M on 4 May;
     max in Jul of 7 on 29th; 3 on 6 Aug; max in Sep of 26 on 19th; max in Oct of 21
     on 5th; max in Nov of 7 on 6th; 11 on 20 Dec (DT, DMB, GO). Skinflats: 6 on 20
     Jan; 12 on 18 Feb; 11 on 17 Mar; 5 on 9 Dec (MVB). Blackness: 22 on 17 Feb; 6 on
     10 Aug; 4 still 2 Sep (AD). 13 Bo'ness 29 Sep (DT).
Additions form 2006: Kinneil: 11 on 21 Sep, 21 on 29 Oct, 27 on 26 Nov (DT).
LONG-TAILED DUCK *Clangula hyemalis* (w)
F   F Skinflats from previous year to 22 Apr with second bird 18-23 Feb and 24-27
     Mar; 4 F on 20 Apr (GO, CJP, MVB *et al.*). F Forth/Clyde Canal, Bonnybridge 21
     Jan and 17 Feb (AA).
S   F Lake of Menteith 21 Jan (NB).
COMMON SCOTER *Melanitta nigra*
F   F Kinneil on 25 Feb and 22 Mar; M there on 2 and 9 Aug (DT, GO).
Addition from 2006: 10 Kinneil 10 Jul (DT).

VELVET SCOTER *Melanitta fusca*
Addition from 2006: F/imm Kinneil 26 Nov (DT).
*BARROW'S GOLDENEYE *Bucephala islandica*
S   M, found on 19 Nov 2006, continued to commute between the R Teith and Eas
     Gobhain, Callander and L Venachar until 27 Apr (NB *et al.*). This has been
     accepted by the BBRC as the first for the Upper Forth area and third for
     Scotland (and Britain). The BBRC noted that this may be a returning bird first
     seen on the Ythan Estuary in May 2005.
GOLDENEYE *Bucephala clangula* (W)
     Inland WeBS counts: 471 in Jan, 557 in Feb, 450 in Mar, 6 in Sep, 30 in Oct, 381
     in Nov, 457 in Dec.
     Forth Est (WeBS) Jan to Mar max: 78 on 28 Jan; Sep to Dec max: 57 on 9 Dec.
F   Site max: 36 Kincardine Br 23 Feb; 25 Skinflats 9 Dec; 23 Kinneil 20 Jan; 14
     Drumbowie Res 6 Feb.
C   Site max: 62 Cambus-Tullibody Br 20 Feb; 48 Gartmorn Dam 20 Jan; 35 R Devon,
     Menstrie 20 Feb.
S   Site max: 101 Lake of Menteith 8 Mar; 63 L Venachar 25 Feb; 35 L Dochart 24 Jan;
     28 Teith-Forth conf 21 Jan; 27 L Ard 24 Jan; 25 Carron Valley Res 18 Feb.
SMEW *Mergus albellus* (w)
S   One redhead Cambusmore 8 Jan, 6 Mar, 26 Mar, 8 Apr and 26 Apr (NB, DT).
RED-BREASTED MERGANSER *Mergus serrator* (B, W)
     Forth Est (WeBS) Jan to Mar max: 73 on 20 Jan; Sep to Dec max: 106 on 7 Oct.
C   2 Cambus 8 Feb; 1 on 20 Mar; 1 on 30 Dec. 1 Kersiepow 13 Feb. 2 F Manorneuk
     18 Feb. Pr Blackdevon Wetlands 20 Mar. 2 Blackgrange 25 Mar. 1 Devonmouth
     Pool 7 Dec.
S   3 Craigforth, R Forth 14 Jan; 6 on 17 Feb; 2 on 11 Dec. 1 Cambusmore 6 Mar. 1
     pr L Katrine 5 May. 2 L Tay 12 May. 2 Ashfield 3 Jun.
GOOSANDER *Mergus merganser* (B, W)
     Inland WeBS counts: 122 in Jan, 152 in Feb, 123 in Mar, 46 in Sep, 50 in Oct, 112
     in Nov, 145 in Dec.
     Forth Est (WeBS) Jan to Mar max: 19 on 20 Jan; Sep to Dec max: 15 on 15 Sep.
F   Site max: 14 Skinflats 15 Sep; 13 Kinneil 24 Aug; 10 Greencraigs Pool 25 Mar; 9
     Union Canal 17 Feb and 15 Dec.
C   Site max: 16 Cambus Pools 17 Sep; 13 Tillicoultry, R Devon 19 Dec; 7
     Blackgrange 18 Feb.
S   Site max: 16 Airthrey Loch 8 Jan; 12 Allan-Teith conf, R Forth 21 Jan; 9 G Finglas
     Res 11 Nov.
RED KITE *Milvus milvus* (b, W)
     5 birds recorded on BBS (previous annual range: 0 - 11 birds).
S   Breeding: 26 AOT; 20 prs laid eggs, 15 successfully fledging 35 Y (DOE, DJC).
     Other sightings: 1 BoA 30 Jan (CL), 2 Dunblane 25 Aug (CJP); 1 Dunblane 2 Nov
     (RS); 1 Kinbuck 5 Nov (DK); 29 Argaty 7 Nov (CT).
WHITE-TAILED EAGLE *Haliaeetus albicilla*
S   Imm from the reintroduction scheme to Tay estuary seen at Flanders Moss 27
     Sep (DAP) and radiotracked around Argaty area in Nov and Dec (KD).
*MARSH HARRIER *Circus aeruginosus* (p)
S   Imm Waterside, BoD 15 Aug (DOE). 1 M Invertrossachs 11 Sep (DOE).
HEN HARRIER *Circus cyaneus* (b, w)
F   M and F Slamannan area 6 and 28 Dec (TF, BGAG).
C   F Blackdevon wetlands 10 Jan, 22 Jan and 6 Feb (CJH). M G Devon 16 Oct.
S   Present in BoD throughout year, especially in winter, with M and F in Autumn
     (KD). M Kippen 16 Jan (DAC). 1 Lecropt Carse 20 Jan (RSx). Ringtail Flanders

Moss 31 Jan; 3 on 18 Feb; M on 6 Mar; M on 15 Sep; M and F in Nov and Dec (DAP, ACR, DK). 1 Callander 17 Feb (RE). M Kinbuck 18 Feb (CJP). 1 Thornhill Carse 6 Mar; 1 on 18 and 29 Dec (DK, PAL). Pr Touch Res 7 Mar (ES). F Brecklinn 7 Dec (DOE). F Kippen Muir Dam 10 Dec (DAC).

*GOSHAWK Accipiter gentilis
S   1 Mill of Argaty, BoD 11 Nov (CJP).

SPARROWHAWK *Accipiter nisus* (B, W)
    7 birds recorded on BBS (previous annual range: 1-6).
F   Records from: Airth; Kinneil; Skinflats (bred); Wallacestone; Borrowstoun.
C   Records from: Alva; Menstrie; Tullibody; Tillicoultry; Cambus; Gartmorn; Coalsnaughton.
S   Records from: Plean; Blairlogie; Stirling; Airthrey; BoA; Braes of Doune; Dunblane; Sheriffmuir; Callander; Gargunnock; Carron Valley Res; Killin; Inverlochlarig; Lanrick (bred).

BUZZARD *Buteo buteo* (B, W)
    BBS: recorded at 0.3 b/1km, slightly below the annual mean.
S   Breeding: 139 prs in 151 territories checked; 92 prs fledged 173$^+$ Y (DOE, DJC).

GOLDEN EAGLE *Aquila chrysaetos* (b, w)
S   2 Stùc a' Chroin 6 Feb (JGR). Sub-ad M BoD 30 Jul (KD).

OSPREY *Pandion haliaetus* (B)
C   1 Tillicoultry Glen 12 May (CVW).
S   Breeding: of 16 prs 14 laid eggs, 12 successfully fledging 24$^+$ Y (DOE, DA, RAB). First record: 1 Doune 31 Mar. Other records from: L Tay in Apr and May; L Rusky from 6 Apr; Lake of Menteith on 7 Apr (2), 20 May (3), 17 Jun and 17 Aug; L Venachar on 11 Apr; L Dochart on 13 Apr; Flanders Moss on 25 Apr; Carron Valley Res on 26 Apr; Callander on 18 Jun; 1-2 Lecropt Carse in Jun; 2 Cambusbarron on 7 Jul; 1 Touch on 7 Jul.

KESTREL *Falco tinnunculus* (B, W)
    4 birds recorded on BBS (previous annual range: 3 - 13 birds).
F   Bred at Skinflats: brood of 2 on 15 Aug. Other records: Fallin; Kinneil; Falkirk; Bonnybridge; Castlecary; Shotts.
C   Records from: Blackgrange; Blackdevon Wetlands; Menstrie; Tullibody; Alva; Alloa; Fishcross; Gartmorn Dam.
S   3 prs bred BoD. Other records: Dunblane; Lecropt; Stirling; Thornhill Carse; Gogar; Cocksburn Res; Kippen; Gargunnock; Killin.

MERLIN *Falco columbarius* (b?, w)
F   M Skinflats 27 Apr. F/imm Skinflats 4 Nov (AB). Imm M Skinflats - Kincardine Br 11 and 18 Nov (MVB, DMB). 1 flew into shop window at Carronshore 16 Nov (AB).
C   1 Slamannan 21 Feb (RS). 1 Tullibody Inch 20 Oct (DMB).
S   Seen throughout year at BoD, with juv present Jul-Sep (KD). Ad M Lecropt Carse 3 Mar (CJH). 1 M S Kirklane, Blairdrummond Moss 10 Mar (DT).

HOBBY *Falco subbuteo*
S   1 Lecropt Carse 20 Jun (DMB). One > W over Uamh Mhòr, BoD 2 Aug (KD).

PEREGRINE *Falco peregrinus* (B, W)
F   Breeding: 1 pr Grangemouth with birds present in area throughout year. Other records: 1 Dunipace in Jan.
C   1 Blackgrange 5 Feb. 1 Devonmouth Pool 9 Apr. 1 Menstrie-Tillicoultry May and Jun.
S   Single birds at: Flanders Moss 17 Jan, 17 Oct, 26 Oct and 11 Dec; Watston 11 Feb; Nether Carse 23 Mar; Airthrey 2 and 13 Apr; M BoA 15 May; M Argaty 17 Sep; Gargunnock 11 Dec. 2 Gillies Hill, Stirling 5 Dec.

RED GROUSE   *Lagopus lagopus*   (B, W)
   BBS: 5 recorded, similar to annual mean.
S   69 Cringate Muir 16 Dec (CJP). 2 Stùc a' Chroin 6 Feb (JGR).
*PTARMIGAN   *Lagopus muta*
S   2 Ben More 4 Apr at 1050m a.s.l. (JT).
BLACK GROUSE   *Tetrao tetrix*   (B, W)
C   1 male recorded (CSBGCG).
S   From the basis of on-going monitoring since 1998 by CSBGCG, evidence
      suggests there are roughly 40 leks in the Stirling Council area, supporting
      around 180 cocks. In 2007, lek size ranged from 20 down to 1, with a mean lek
      size of 4.5. Trends in lek size vary but some evidence is beginning to suggest
      that the rapid rate of decline over recent years in numbers and range has
      slowed. Strongholds remain in the Campsies and SW L Tay, with significant
      increases around L Katrine.
GREY PARTRIDGE   *Perdix perdix*   (B, W)
      2 birds recorded on BBS (previous annual range: 0 - 8 birds).
F   Skinflats: pr Feb-May; max was 20 on 4 Nov (AB, MVB, AET). 2 Airth 20 Mar
      (AET). 8 Kerdieshill Fm Maddiston 25 Feb (MWO).
C   Site max: 2 Blackdevon Wetlands 20 Mar (CJH); 9 R Devon, Alva 13 Feb (DAC).
      5 Tullibody 8 Dec (DAC).
S   2 Carbrook Mains, Plean 27 Jun (JF).
*QUAIL   *Coturnix coturnix*
S   M Gartmorn Dam 21 May (DT). M Blairdrummond Moss 22 May (JRC).
PHEASANT   *Phasianus colchicus*   (B, W)
      BBS: recorded at 0.5 b/1km, similar to the annual mean. Very large numbers
      released on shooting estates, otherwise widespread but in small numbers.
WATER RAIL   *Rallus aquaticus*   (b, w)
F   1 Kinneil 6 Feb (RS). Skinflats: 1 on 9 Feb; 2 on 9 Mar; 1 in Aug-Nov with 2 on 6
      Oct (DAC, GO, GG, RS).
C   2 Blackgrange 21 Jan (ACC). 1 Tullibody Inch 3 Mar and 26 Nov (DMB).
S   2 Upper Taylorton-Fallin, R Forth 21 Jan (ACC). 3 Easter L of Daldorn 18 Feb
      (BB). F Gartmore Curling Pond 23 May (RW). 1 Polmaise Lagoons 18 Oct and 23
      Nov (DAC).
MOORHEN   *Gallinula chloropus*   (B, W)
      Inland WeBS counts: 118 in Jan, 125 in Feb, 90 in Mar, 106 in Sep, 142 in Oct, 156
      in Nov, 153 in Dec.
F   Site max: 18 Forth/Clyde Canal, Bonnybridge 9 Dec; 17 Callendar Park, Falkirk
      21 Jan; 10 Kinneil House 25 Mar; 10 Millhall Res, Polmont 20 Feb; 9 St Helen's
      Loch, Bonnybridge 1 Oct.
C   Site max: 6 Cambus Pools 16 Nov; 5 Gartmorn Dam in Jan and Feb.
S   Breeding: pr and 2 Y L Venachar 29 Jul; 10 Y Torrielochan 15 Aug; pr and 4 Y
      Castle Park, Stirling 1 Oct; 1-3 prs bred Airthrey Loch. Site max: 19 Airthrey
      Loch 7 Nov; 10 Vale of Coustry; 6 Doune Ponds 23 Jan.
COOT   *Fulica atra*   (B, W)
      Inland WeBS counts: 287 in Jan, 213 in Feb, 151 in Mar, 107 in Sep, 159 in Oct,
      224 in Nov, 259 in Dec.
F   Ad Kinneil 29 Jul.
C   Breeding: pr Cambus Village Pool in Apr and May; pr with 3 Y and 1 ON
      Naemoor Pond 12 Jun. Site max: 174 Gartmorn Dam 20 Jan.
S   Breeding: 15 ON Airthrey Loch 30 Mar; pr with 5 Y Polmaise Lagoons 25 May,
      3 Y on 30 Jul. Pr with 3 Y Cambusmore 8 Jul, 1 Y on 15 Aug; 1 Y Ochlochy Pond,
      Dunblane 28 Sep. Site max: 77 Aithrey Loch 22 Oct; 47 Lake of Menteith 17 Dec.

OYSTERCATCHER *Haematopus ostralegus* (B, W)
    WeBS Forth estuary peaks were 397 Feb and 223 Oct.
F   Return inland: 3 Fallin 6 Feb; 1 Bo'ness Walk 18 Feb. There were no counts from Skinflats in the early part of the year. 35 birds returned there 8 Jun with 106 there 2 Aug and 79 on 25 Oct. 94 Kinneil 2 Aug was the only count of note at that location. 35 Blackness 10 Aug.
C   Return inland: 17 around Cambus Pools 5 Feb with 39 there 17 Feb. 25 on newly excavated pool at Blackdevon Wetlands 21 Feb with 43 there 26 Feb. Similar counts at Blackdevon with maxima of 30 on 17 Mar, 35 on 20 Mar, 11 on 16 Apr and 11 on 31 May. Elsewhere 8 on R Devon at Alva 2 Apr; up to 10 Devonmouth Pool 13 Apr. 1 bird alarm-called from roof of old Coop building in Alloa 18 Apr. 2 prs bred at Castlebridge Business Park, Forestmill: 1 pr raised 1 Y, outcome of other pr unknown, 1 Y killed by crow.
S   Return inland: 11 Craigforth 6 Jan with 44 there 14 Jan and ca 230 on 13 Mar. 1 Doune and 4 Airthrey 30 Jan with up to 6 at latter location to Jul. 5 Cocksburn Res, BoA 2 Feb with 36 there 14 Mar; 10 Gart, Callander 3 Feb; 37 R Forth, Nether Carse and 38 Ashfield 26 Feb with 81 at latter locality 12 Mar. 58 L Walton also 12 Mar. 12 L Dochart 13 Apr. Pr nested Duckburn Park Industrial Estate, Dunblane. 2 AOT Cambusmore GP. 1 Craigforth 20 Nov is thought to have wintered (DT).
*LITTLE RINGED PLOVER *Charadrius dubius*
F   1 Skinflats 14 Apr (ACC). Pr Gart GP 26 and 27 Apr were display fighting and copulating, 1 still there at probable nest site 15 May but site bulldozed by 20 Jun (DT). These are the 12th and 13th records, respectively, for the area since modern recording began in 1974.
    Addition from 2006: M 10 Apr to 30 May Gart GP displayed 5 May but no F ever seen (DT).
RINGED PLOVER *Charadrius hiaticula* (b, W)
C   Up to 7 on newly excavated pool at Blackdevon Wetlands 21 Feb to 1 May giving display calls in Mar; 1 AOT assumed (CJH). 4 Cambus Village Pool 14 May.
F   As in 2006, much smaller numbers than before. 12 Kinneil 25 Mar with 16 there 28 Oct. 7 Skinflats 20 May with 2 there 10 Jul, 21 on 24 Aug, 10 on 29 Aug, 5 at the Carron mouth on 15 Sep and 4 on 9 Dec. 31 Kincardine Br 30 May.
S   2 L Tay, Killin throughout Apr. Pr Touch Res 16 Apr, 26 May and 9 Jul. 1 L Venachar 27 Apr. 2 Gart GP 26 Apr with 5$^+$ there 15 May, 1 confirmed and 1 probable nest on 5 Jun but site bulldozed by 20 Jun.
*DOTTEREL *Charadrius morinellus* (p)
S   3 Ben Ledi 12 May (FCS).
GOLDEN PLOVER *Pluvialis apricaria* (B, W)
    WeBS estuary peaks were very low in the first part of the year with max of only 8 birds in Jan but 1001 in Oct.
F   Another poor year. 150 Slamannan 4 Jan. 22 flying over former peat works, Darnrigg Moss 23 Feb. 22 Kinneil 14 Feb; ca. 53 there 25 Feb included 2 northern race birds in breeding plumage. Return to the estuary was not noted until 1 Skinflats 12 Aug with 30 there 26 Aug and 20 on 29 Oct. At Kinneil 5 on 14 Sep, rising to 17 on 19th, 253 on 29th dropping to 25 on 6 Nov and 110 on 31 Dec. 132 Kincardine Br 15 Sep rose to a max 570 on 7 Oct.
S   6 Balquhidder 25 Mar. 22 BoD, Drumloist 20 Apr. 3-5 AoT at BoD, Uamh Beg-Slymaback.
GREY PLOVER *Pluvialis squatarola* (W)
F   18 Kinneil 14 Feb with 2 there 2 Oct. 1 Blackness 17 Feb. 1 Skinflats 29 Aug with

48 there 25 Oct and 6 on 23 Nov. 2 Bo'ness 29 Sep. 3 Carriden 23 Nov.

LAPWING *Vanellus vanellus* (B, W)
WeBS estuary peaks were 447 in Jan and 1942 in Oct.

F   Flocks were down. 190 on the Skinflats estuary on 20 Jan was a poor showing. 300 there on 15 Sep, 805 on 7 Oct and 140 on 11 Nov were also small compared to previous years. An ad with 3 chicks at Skinflats itself on 25 Feb was very early, 25 there on 8 Jun included 2 downy chicks, 250$^+$ on 26 Aug and 225 on 29 Oct. Ca 350 Kinneil 9 Aug with ca 500 there 24 Aug, 300 on 1 Oct and 400 on 31 Dec were also comparatively small flocks.

C   48 on newly excavated pool at Blackdevon Wetlands 2 Feb rose to 92 on 21 Feb with 39 still on 2 Mar; there were up to 12 AoT between Mar and May; good numbers in Oct saw a max of 120 on 23rd (CJH). 260 flew upstream at Haugh of Blackgrange 18 Feb. 18 along R Devon Alva-Menstrie 4 Mar with 230 there 11 Sep. 1 AoT Blackdevonmouth 27 Apr. 2 prs with 3 chicks Menstrie Br 11 May and 26 Jun. 700 Tullibody Inch 5 Nov.

S   80 Netherton, Thornhill 5 Jan. Ca 300 Carse of Lecropt 21 Jan. 450 nr Polmaise 20 Feb. 4 prs Doune Lodge, BoD 6 Apr and 3 prs there at Drumloist 15 May. 3 prs Hill of Row 13 May. 150 Muir Park Fm, L Coulter 9 Jul. 300 nr SE of Flanders Moss 2 Nov with 50 there 11 Dec.

KNOT *Calidris canutus* (W)
WeBS estuary peaks were 2840 in Jan and 505 in Dec.

F   The peak of the winter/spring period was 2800 Kincardine Br 20 Jan. 6 G Artney 25 Jan (RSx). 22 Blackness 17 Feb. 4 Kinneil 31 Mar with ad and 5 juvs there 30 Aug, ca 110 on 29 Sep, 1300 on 23 Nov (most at Bo'ness) and 1000$^+$ on 23 Dec. Up to 3 birds Jan to Aug at Skinflats with 40 there 29 Aug and 107 on 25 Oct.

SANDERLING *Calidris alba*
F   1 Tullibody Inch 26 May and 1 Kincardine Br 30 May (DMB).

*LITTLE STINT *Calidris minuta*
F   1 Skinflats 9 Sep (BRG). 2 Kinneil 5 Oct (DT). 1 Kincardine Br 13 Oct (CJP, BD).

CURLEW SANDPIPER *Calidris ferruginea* (p)
Much smaller numbers than in 2006.

F   1 Skinflats 20 May with 2 there 27 Jul, 2 on 2 Aug, 1 on 30 Sep and 1 on 25 Oct (GO, AB, MVB).

Autumn passage, area summary (minimum number/half month)							
Jul		Aug		Sep		Oct	
0	2	2	0	0	1	0	1

*PURPLE SANDPIPER *Calidris maritima* (w)
F   1 Kinneil 11 Nov (JRC).

DUNLIN *Calidris alpina* (b?, W)
WeBS estuary peaks were much lower than in 2006 with 3792 in Feb and 1750 in Nov.

F   Much lower numbers than in 2006. 1455 Skinflats 20 Jan with 1210 there 18 Feb. 40 there 20 Jul rising to 140 on 24 Aug, 992 on 7 Oct, 1105 on 11 Nov and 1474 on 9 Dec. 302 Kinneil 28 Oct.

C   10 R Forth, Alloa Inches 18 Feb. In May up to 14 in breeding plumage Cambus Village Pool.

S   4 L Tay, Killin 22 Apr.

RUFF *Philomachus pugnax* (w, p)
F   As in 2006 one bird overwintered at Skinflats where it was seen repeatedly between 27 Jan and 1 Mar (ACC,AB, DAC, MVB, RS). A single on spring passage (same bird?) was present 31 Mar to 24 Apr (GO, DAC, RS, ACC, AET). Autumn

passage started with 7 on 14 Aug rising to 9-13 between 24 and 30 Aug, then dropped to between 3 to 8 between 4 and 9 Sep (DOE, MVB, GG, AB, DMB, AET). An overwintering bird was seen repeatedly between 31 Oct and 29 Dec (AB, MVB, GO, DMB, GG). 1-2 Kinneil 24 to 30 Aug (DMB, MVB, DT, RDZ).

C Single Cambus/Cambus Village Pools 22 Apr to 23 May with 2 there 7 May (CJP, DH, NB, AET, JRC).

Autumn passage, area summary (minimum number/half month)							
Jul		Aug		Sep		Oct	
0	0	0	13	8	0	0	1

JACK SNIPE *Lymnocryptes minimus* (w)
F 5 Kinneil 6 Feb with 2 there 23 Dec (RS).
C Singles Blackgrange, Cambus 21 Jan, Pool of Muckhart community woodland 4 Feb and Kennet Pans 18 Nov (ACC, DT, DMB).
S Singles Flanders Moss 9 Jan, 1 and 30 Nov; Netherton and R Forth, Carse of Lecropt 17 Feb, Kinbuck 8 Oct (DAP, DT).

SNIPE *Gallinago gallinago* (B,W)
   Estuary WeBS: no records.
F 12 Gilston, Falkirk 16 Apr. 9 Skinflats 24 Aug with 14 there 25 Aug and 8 on 29 Aug; 5 on the saltmarsh there 4 Nov. 71 Kincardine B 13 Oct.
C 15 nr Haugh, W of Dollar 3 Nov. 5 Castlebridge Business Park, Forestmill 7 Nov.
S 10 Flanders Moss 24 Feb with 5 there 22 Mar. 2 Strathfillan 14 Apr. Single drumming Sheriffmuir 14 May and chipping Townhead, Gargunnock Hills 20 May. 8 Carron Res 8 Oct. 6 Ashfield Pools 11 Nov.

WOODCOCK *Scolopax rusticola* (B, W)
   Grossly under-recorded during the breeding season.
F 1 Westfield, Airth 20 Mar (AET).
C Roding birds: 2 E of Coalsnaughton 30 Mar (JT). Single nr Devonknowes and 1 or 2 nr Lawmuir 26 May. 1 Dollarbeg and 2 Boar Wood, Aberdona 31 May. Single School Wood, Forestmill 5 Jun. 1-3 Brucefield and 2 N of Brucefield 8 Jun (DT).
S Singles Flanders Moss 10 Jan, 15 Feb, 22 Mar, 7 and 30 Nov, 11 Dec (2) and 12 Dec (DAP). Singles Lanrick 14 Jan, BoD wind farm 14 Feb; Lecropt 15 Feb; L Tay, Killin 1 to 18 Apr; BoD, Kilbryde 2 Dec, Dunblane 8 Dec (DOE, KD, CJP, JPH).

BLACK-TAILED GODWIT *Limosa limosa* (W)
   WeBS estuary peaks were low with 34 Feb and 234 Nov.
F Present most year in the Grangemouth area. Monthly peaks at Kinneil: 1 Jan (20th), 263 Apr (22nd), 2 May (30th), 51 Jul (10th), 223 Aug (20th), 197 Sep (14th), 219 Oct (28th), 200 Nov (7th) and 150 Dec (9th). Generally smaller numbers but higher peaks at Skinflats: 1 Jan (26th), 9 Mar (17th), 419 Apr (21st) - this was accompanied by an influx of islandica birds with up to 60 of this race on 19th and up to ca 620 on 24th Apr -, 12 May (8th), 2 Jun (24th), 38 Jul (23rd), 68 Aug (16th), 2 Sep (4th), 1 Oct (29th). Elsewhere 25 S Alloa 16 Jan.
C Increasing numbers are found upstream of Kincardine Br in spring. 33 on newly excavated pool Blackdevon Wetlands 13 Feb with 22 on 2 Mar dropping to 1 by 30 Mar. At Cambus/Cambus Village Pool 52 on 30 Mar rose to 73 on 11 Apr, 157 on 21 Apr and 200 on 22 Apr. In May numbers steadied to between 11 and 25; this included birds in breeding plumage. At Devonmouth Pool 61 on 6 Apr (ca half in breeding plumage) rose to 104 on 18 Apr and ca 425 on 23 Apr. 75 Tullibody Inch 15 Apr. These do not seem to be birds moving here from the Grangemouth area, at least in April when numbers there were higher than in 2006.
S 34 Dunmore 23 Feb. 1 L Tay, Killin 22 Apr.

BAR-TAILED GODWIT *Limosa lapponica* (W)
Webs estuary peaks were 160 in Feb and 37 in Nov.
F   Numbers were again low at Kinneil with isolated, larger peaks and very low at
Skinflats. 2 Kinneil 2 Jan with 45 there 10 Mar, 150 on 23 Dec and 25 on 29 Dec.
16 Blackness 23 Sep. 2 Skinflats 20 Apr and 1 on 22 Apr.
C   4 Alloa Inch 29 Aug.
WHIMBREL *Numenius phaeopus* (p)
F   Poor spring and autumn passages. Spring: single at Skinflats 22 Apr with 4 there
13 May and 2 on 20 May (ACC, AB, GO). Autumn: singles Kinneil 10 and 29 Jul
with 5 there 9 Aug, 1 on 17, 2 on 23 and 1 on 30 Aug (DT, GO). 2 Skinflats 6 and
24 Jul and 1 on 16 Aug (GO, DOE).
S   1 L Tay, Killin on 7, 8 and 13 May (JPH).

Autumn passage, area summary (minimum number/half month)							
Jul		Aug		Sep		Oct	
3	3	5	2	0	0	0	0

CURLEW *Numenius arquata* (B, W)
Webs estuary peaks were 1181 Jan and 1144 Dec.
F   Skinflats estuary: 599 on 20 Jan, 315 there 18 Feb, 363 on 7 Oct, 247 on 11 Nov
and 271 on 9 Dec. The ponds themselves held 150 birds on 26 Jan and 85 on 26
Mar. Max at Kinneil: 2 in Feb, 15 in Mar, ca 600 in Jul, 569 in Aug and 15 in Nov,
while 515 was the WebS estuary max. in Sep. Elsewhere 487 Kincardine Br 5 Jan,
ca 220 Airth 31 Jan. 141 Blackness 17 Feb and 62 Gilston, Falkirk 26 Feb.
C   120 Devonmouth Pool 16 Jan with 120 in Cambus (Village) Pools area 21 Jan, 200
on 22 Jan, 140 on 8 Feb and 98 on 18 Dec. Up to 30 on newly excavated pool at
Blackdevon Wetlands in Mar with 4 still there 1 May. 300 Blackgrange 5 Feb and
ca 450 there 4 Mar. 2 Gartmorn Dam 27 Jun.
S   Spring return: 92 Carse of Lecropt 13 Mar, 2 displaying Flanders Moss 27 Apr.
During breeding season Cringate Muir; King's Park, Stirling and Carse of
Lecropt.
*SPOTTED REDSHANK *Tringa erythropus* (p)
F   Single Kinneil 6 Feb and 13 Mar (RS).
Addition from 2006: juv Kinneil 11 to 21 Sep (DT).
REDSHANK *Tringa totanus* (B, W)
Webs estuary peaks were down with 1723 Jan and 2048 Oct.
F   Estuary counts at Skinflats: 1093 in Jan, 476 in Feb, 397 in Mar, 707 in Sep, 947 in
Oct, 338 in Nov and 1078 in Dec. The pools held 340 birds 2 Aug and 555 on 25
Oct. Kinneil max were: 80 in Apr, 44 in Jul, 1220 in Aug, 1017 in Sep (WebS) and
400 in Oct.
C   A single at Blackdevon Wetlands 17 Mar increased to 4 by month end (display
calling noted). Up to 7 birds there Apr and May - 1 displaying pr (CJH). Singles
Devonmouth Pool 6 and 9 Apr and Cambus Village Pool 9 Apr.
S   2 L Walton 12 Mar; 2 Carse of Lecropt 13 Mar. 2-3 Gart GP 8 Apr, 13 and 27 May
and 17 Jun. 28 L Tay, Killin 22 Apr; 1 Carron Valley Res 26 Apr and 3
Blairdrummond Moss 30 Apr.
GREENSHANK *Tringa nebularia* (w, p)
Webs estuary counts: 4 in Jan, 5 in Nov.
F   Skinflats: up to 3 birds in Jan dropped to 2 in Feb and Mar. A bird during the
2nd part of Apr may have been the same or a bird on passage (CJP, MVB, AB,
ACC, DAC, CJH, GO). Autumn return started with a single 29 Jun, rising to 6 in
Jul. Aug max 7 birds on 7th and 16th and 5 on 28th (AET, GO, JT, AB, MVB, ACC,
RS, DOE, RDZ). Up to 3 birds in Sep and Oct dropped to 2 in Nov and 1 in Dec

(AB, RS, MVB, DMB, GG). Kinneil: single between 25 Feb and 5 Apr (DT). 2 in Nov and early Dec with a single at the R Avon mouth in late Dec (RS, DMB, AET, GO). Elsewhere singles Polmaise lagoons 20 Sep, S Alloa 23 Sep and 2 Kincardine Br 4 Oct (CJM, DAC, DMB)

C   1 Devonmouth Pool 11 Apr had red ring on left leg (NB).

S   2 L Tay, Killin 6 and 7 Apr with at least 1 there 11, 16 and 18 Apr (JPH).

Autumn passage, area summary (minimum number/half month)							
Jul		Aug		Sep		Oct	
6	2	7	5	3	3	5	0

GREEN SANDPIPER *Tringa ochropus* (w, p)

This species now occurs as a wintering bird in small numbers as well as a passage migrant.

F   Singles R Carron, Caronshore-Skinflats 15 Jan stayed from 2006. Single R Avon, Grangemouth 9 Feb. Single Gilston, Falkirk 9-15 Mar (AB, RS). 2 Muirdyke Burn, Skinflats 26 Aug with 1 at Skinflats 4 and 29 Aug (AB, DMB, GO).

S   Single Allan Water, Kinbuck 18 Feb and 8 Oct (BD, CJP). Single R Forth, Nether Carse 26 Feb with 2 there 23 Mar (ACR).

WOOD SANDPIPER *Tringa glareola* (p)

F   1 Skinflats 12 and 15 May (GO, BRG). This is the 18th record for the recording area.

COMMON SANDPIPER *Tringa hypoleucos* (B)

F   Singles R Carron at Carronshore 20 Apr and at Dunipace 18 May. Kinneil: 1 on 24 Apr and 6 and 10 Jul with 5 there 17 Jul. Skinflats: 1 on 14 May and 24 Jun with up to 4 there between late Jun and early Aug and 1 thereafter until 27 Aug.

C   2 Cambus 22 Apr with 1 there 10 Aug. 1 Gartmorn Dam 27 Jun.

S   Spring passage: singles L Tay, Killin 18 Apr; Kinbuck Br 19 Apr; 2 Carron Valley Res 26 Apr; 4 Lake of Menteith 26 Apr and 2 L Venachar 27 Apr. During breeding season reported from: R Teith, Kilmahog and Callander (7 birds); Gart GP (up to 6 birds); Inverlochlarig; Stronachlachar (3 birds); Allan Water, Dunblane and Cocksburn Res.

Autumn passage, area summary (minimum number/half month)							
Jun		Jul		Aug		Sep	
1	4	5	6	2	1	0	0

*SPOTTED SANDPIPER *Actitis macularia*

F   Ad winter R Avon mouth, Kinneil 24 Dec to year end (RS, GO). This is the first record for our recording area. This bird proved initially elusive but once its movements had been determined - it tended to favour the upper reaches of the Avon but when these became submerged at high tide it made its way down to the river mouth - it became comparatively easy to connect with, on occasions showing down to a few metres.

TURNSTONE *Arenaria interpres* (W)

F   4 Kinneil 14 and 20 Jan with 5 there 25 Feb and 1 in breeding plumage 24 Apr (ACC, DT); 2 there 6 Aug, 1 on 5 Oct, 2 on 23 Nov, 1 on 24 and 28 Dec and 2 on 30 Dec (DMB, DT, GO, RSW, DM). 1 R Carron mouth, Skinflats 18 Feb with 4 on 17 Mar and 3 on 7 Oct (MVB). Elsewhere: 1 Blackness 17 Feb with 6 there 5 Oct (DK, DAC). 4 Grangepans 14 Sep. 1 Carriden 23 Nov (MVB, DMB).

Spotted Sandpiper at Kinneil
The decurved, pink-based bill (here showing pale) and pale legs show well in this photo.
Photo by John Nadin

ARCTIC SKUA *Stercorarius parasiticus* (p)
F   Kinneil: 1 on 5 Sep; 1 on 10 Sep; 2 on 13 Sep; 11 on 14 Sep; 1 on 19 Sep (DT,
        DMB). 3 Skinflats 24 Sep (CJP, BD). 3 Bo'ness 29 Sep (DT). Singles Blackness and
        Kinneil 5 Oct (DAC, DT). 1 Dunmore 7 Oct (DAC). 4 Kincardine Br 13 Oct (CJP,
        BD). 1 Skinflats 25 Oct (MVB).
GREAT SKUA *Stercorarius skua*
F   1 Skinflats 24 Sep (CJP, BD).
LITTLE GULL *Larus minutus*
F   First summer bird Skinflats 24 Jun (AB).
C   Imm Blackdevon Wetlands 26 Jun (CJH).
*MEDITERRANEAN GULL *Larus melanocephalus*
F   Ad Kinneil 6 Nov (DM, MT). This is the 12th record for the recording area since
        1974.
BLACK-HEADED GULL *Larus ridibundus* (B, W)
        Inland WeBS counts: 653 in Jan, 955 in Feb, 593 in Mar, 264 in Sep, 521 in Oct,
        1186 in Nov, 1069 in Dec.
        BBS: recorded at 0.3 b/1km, below the annual mean.
F   Max counts: 325 Blackness 10 Aug.
C   Max counts: 1550 Blackdevon Wetlands 2 Feb; 242 Gartmorn Dam 29 Jan.
*RING-BILLED GULL *Larus delawarensis*
F   Ad Kinneil 28 Oct, 4 Nov and 30 Dec (DT, GG, KH *et al.*). This may have been
        the returning bird from 2005 and 2006. This record is still to be validated by the

BBRC and will be the 3nd record for the area since modern recording began in 1974, if accepted.

COMMON GULL *Larus canus* (B,W)

Inland WeBS counts: 929 in Jan, 613 in Feb, 597 in Mar, 22 in Sep, 165 in Oct, 321 in Nov, 256 in Dec.

BBS: recorded at 0.7 b/1km, below the annual mean.

C   Summer: 6 Blackdevon Wetlands 26 Jun.

S   Breeding: 9 ON Cambusmore 13 May; pr BoD May but failed. Other records: 277 King's Park, Stirling 22 Sep.

LESSER BLACK-BACKED GULL *Larus fuscus* (b, S)

Inland WeBS counts: 9 in Jan, 5 in Feb, 148 in Mar, 34 in Sep, 83 in Oct, 45 in Nov, 8 in Dec.

Forth Est (WeBS) Jan to Mar max: 13 on 17 Mar; Sep to Dec max: 37 on 15 Sep.

F   Max counts: 15 Skinflats 22 Apr and 12 Aug.

C   Max count: 24 Blackdevon Wetlands 26 Jun.

HERRING GULL *Larus argentatus* (b, W)

Inland WeBS counts: 73 in Jan, 376 in Feb, 39 in Mar, 723 in Sep, 106 in Oct, 148 in Nov, 85 in Dec.

C   Max count: 43 Blackdevon Wetlands 16 May.

Addition from 2006: ca 1000 (mostly sub-ads) Kinneil 4 Jun.

GREAT BLACK-BACKED GULL *Larus marinus* (S, W)

Inland WeBS counts: 3 in Jan, 1 in Feb, 2 in Mar, 6 in Sep, 14 in Oct, 4 in Nov, 10 in Dec.

F   Max count: 40 Kinneil 5 Sep.

KITTIWAKE *Rissa tridactyla* (P, w)

F   1 Skinflats 7 Sep (DMB). 480+ Kinneil 14 Sep (DT). 1 Skinflats 24 Sep (CJP, DB). 16 Kinneil 4 Nov (GG).

Addition from 2006 Kinneil: 75 on 4 Apr and 47 on 11 Aug (DT).

SANDWICH TERN *Sterna sandvicensis* (P)

F   11 Kincardine Br 15 Sep. 6 Blackness 23 Sep. 16 Grangemouth and 33 Kincardine Br 7 Oct.

C   2 Tullibody Inch 19 Aug, 10 there 22 Sep.

S   5 Carron Valley Res 3 Jun (DMB).

COMMON TERN *Sterna hirundo* (B)

F   First: 7 at Kinneil 4 May (DT). Skinflats: up to 10 in May on 13th; 14 on 26 Jun; 5 in Jul. Grangemouth: 16 on 2 Aug and 6 on 7 Aug. Blackness: 3 in Sep. Kincardine Br: 2 on 15 Sep and 1 on 7 Oct.

ARCTIC TERN *Sterna paradisaea*

F   2 Skinflats 12 May; 1 still on 13 May (ACC, CJP). 1 Kinneil 13 Sep (DMB). 1 Blackness 23 Sep (AD). 1 Skinflats 4 Oct (DMB).

*BLACK TERN *Chlidonias niger*

F   Juv Kinneil 9 Aug (DT).

GUILLEMOT *Uria aalge* (W)

F   Kinneil: 7 on 14 Sep; 18 on 19 Sep (MVB, DT). 9 Skinflats 24 Sep (CJP, BD). 10 Bo'ness 29 Sep (DT). 2 Kinneil 5 Oct (DT). Kincardine Br: 13 on 7 Oct; 5 on 13 Oct (MVB, CJP, BD).

C   1 R Devon, Cambus 2 Oct (DAC).

RAZORBILL *Alca torda* (w)

F   2 Skinflats 24 Sep (CJP, BD). 11 Bo'ness 29 Sep (DT).

S   1 Fallin, R Forth 28 Sep (AET).

FERAL PIGEON *Columba livia* (B,W)

C   120 Alloa Glassworks disturbed by Kestrel.

STOCK DOVE Columba oenas (B, W)
F   11 Kinneil 25 Feb, 16 there 25 Mar, 14 on 24 Aug and 2 on 11 Oct. 2 Skinflats 20
      Apr, 4 there 22 Apr, 2 (at Howkerse) 24 Apr, 1 on 8 Aug and 36 on 7 Nov. 20
      Gilston, Falkirk 9 May. 46 Powfoulis Manor 7 Oct.
C   2 Woodland Park, Alva 2 Feb. 2 Blackgrange 20 May. 2 Menstrie 26 Mar with 1+
      there 20 May. 1 Gartmorn Dam 27 Jun.
S   Pr BoD, Doune Lodge 9 Apr. 4 Causewayhead, Stirling, and 5 Stirling Br 11 May.
      3 Riverside, Stirling 17 Jun. 2 Fintry 5 Jul.
WOODPIGEON Columba palumbus (B, W)
F   800+ Skinflats 7 Nov.
S   400 Greenyards Fm, Dunblane 11 Nov.
COLLARED DOVE Streptopelia decaocto (B, W)
Greatly under-reported. No significant records were received this year
CUCKOO Cuculus canorus (B)
      Arrival in Apr: Flanders Moss 25th was 4 days later than in 2006 and 4 days later
      than in 2005. This was followed by birds at Darnrig Moss, Gart GP and
      Cocksburn Res 26th; L Tay, Killin; Brig o'Turk and BoD, Bows all on 27th; BoD,
      Argaty 29th and Blairdrummond Moss 30th.
C   1 Muckhart 7 May. 2 Alloa Inch 21 Jun.
S   In May: singles Hermitage Wood, Airthrey 3rd; Cocksburn Res 9th and 16th (2);
      Clash Fm, Callander 12th; Gleann Breac-nic 13th; Carron Valley Res 14th; Tom
      Dubh, Callander and Arndrum, L Ard Forest 20th; 4 in dispute Flanders Moss
      27th. In Jun: 1 G Lochay 6th; 2 Sheriffmuir 13th and 1 Menteith Hills 24th.
BARN OWL Tyto alba (b, w)
S   1 Thornhill Carse 26 and 29 Jan (DK). 1 found dead on the A811 nr Buchlyvie
      29 Jan with other birds there at Kepcelloch 14 Nov and 18 Dec (JT, DK). In
      Dunblane 1 at Keir 28 Mar and 1 throughout year at Kippenross (NB, KD). At
      BoD, 1 at Drumloist 16 May fledged 5 Y and 1 at Uamh Mhor no date. 1
      Blairdrummond 31 Aug (DOE, KD). 2 by nest box at Flanders Moss 30 Nov
      (DAP).
TAWNY OWL Strix aluco (B, W)
F   1 Jaw Fm, Slamannan 15 May. 1-2 Skinflats 24 Sep. 1 Liddle Drive, Bo'ness 20
      Oct.
C   Birds calling at Tait Place, Tillicoultry 18 Mar and on several days in Aug. 2
      calling Gartmorn Dam 28 Apr with 1 there 17 May. 1 West Loaningbank,
      Menstrie 21 May. Pr calling Coalsnaughton 31 May. 1 calling E of Aberdona 5
      Jun. 2 calling Harviestoun old mine 7 Jun.
S   BoA: 1 calling Coneyhill 6 Jan and 1 on 16 Dec. 1 calling Broomridge, Stirling 26
      Jan and 2 there 1 Nov. 1 calling Carron Valley Res 24 Mar. Bird incubating in tree
      Cromlix 8 Apr. 1 L Tay, Killin 18 Apr. 1 dead on A811 at Cambusbarron 18 Apr.
      At BoD: 2 prs bred Argaty 29 Apr and 1 pr bred Dumloist 27 May. Pr bred Doune
      13 May. 1 Lake of Menteith 20 May. 1 Lanrick 26 Jun. 1 dead on A84 nr caravan
      park, Callander 8 Aug. 1 calling Springwood Ave., Stirling 20 to 28 Dec.
LONG-EARED OWL Asio otus (b, w)
F   2 with juv Whitehill, Denny 10 Jun (KMcl)
S   Feathers found BoD wind farm 1 Jan and 7 Mar (KD). 1 Sheriffmuir 8 May and
      9 Jul bred nearby in Perthshire and had 1-2 juvs (DT).
SHORT-EARED OWL Asio flammeus (b, W)
      For this rather local breeder, a more systematic survey of known breeding areas
      and potential breeding sites would be of value.
F   2 Kinneil 20 Jan (GO).
C   5 over R Forth foreshore at Blackdevon Wetlands 22 Jan with up to 4 there in

Feb and 2 on 2 Mar (CJH). These sightings of presumably the same birds represent only the 4th record in Clackmannanshire since 1996.

S   1 Flanders Moss 12 Jan. Remains found at BoD in Feb. 2 hunting Cringate Muir 24 Mar (DAP, KD, AET). Singles hunting Black Hill, Sheriffmuir 1, 20 and 22 May; Earls Hill, Gargunnock Hills 20 May and Forthbank, Stirling 25 Aug (DK, CJH, NB).

SWIFT *Apus apus* (B)

Spring arrival: 3 Gartcows, Falkirk and 20 Kippenross, Dunblane 28 Apr were 1 day earlier than in 2005 and 3 days earlier than in 2006. This was followed by 1 Callander 29 Apr; singles Cambus, BoA and Stirling 2 May; Carron and Blackdevon Wetlands 4 May.

Autumn departure in Aug: 2 Gartmorn Dam 7th. 12 Coneyhill, BoA 8th with 16 there 9th and 2 on 10th which was 18 days earlier than in 2006 and 9 days earlier than in 2005.

C   25 Gartmorn Dam 27 Jun.

S   100 Blairdrummond 13 May. 20 Flanders Moss 20 Jun. Up to 37 Coneyhill, BoA in Jul, presumed hawking ants.

KINGFISHER *Alcedo atthis* (b, w)

F   Kinneil: singles 20 Jan, 19 Oct, 21 Nov, 25 (2), 27 and 31 Dec. R Carron: singles Dunipace 18 May, Carronshore 1 Sep and 13 Dec and Langlees 17 Sep. 2 Skinflats 2 Dec.

C   R Devon: 1 at Cambus 8 Feb with 2 there 4 Apr and 1 on 4 May, 2 Oct, 12 Nov and 28 Dec; singles nr Crook of Devon 1 Apr and Alva-Menstrie 2 and 18 Apr and 11 Sep; nr Taits' Tomb, Tillicoultry 3 Nov.

S   Singles Gart GP 8 Apr, at nearby Keltie Burn 27 Apr, 15 May where maybe nested. R Teith: 2 Callander 12 May, 12 Jun and 2 Inverardoch 17 Jul, 15 Sep. Singles Dunblane 4 Sep, 14 Oct, 8 Dec; R Forth, Carse of Lecropt 5 Sep, 2 Dec; Kinbuck, Ashfield 28 Sep; L Venachar 28 Sep; Polmaise lagoons 18 Oct, 23 Nov; Lanrick 11 Nov.

GREEN WOODPECKER *Picus viridis* (B, W)

More records away from SE needed to establish true status.

F   Single Plean CP 10 Apr.

C   Birds were seen or heard repeatedly in the Harviestoun area of Tillicoultry from late Mar to mid-Jul with other sightings around Tillicoultry 18 Nov and 10 Dec. Elsewhere singles were reported from Alva at Alva Glen 7 Mar; R Devon 2 Apr and Woodland Park 9 Apr. Around Menstrie birds were reported 30 Apr and 6 and 20 May. Single E of Clackmannan 9 Nov.

S   Singles Killin 27 Mar, at L Tay there 1 Apr and at the marshes 15 Dec. 2 BoD, Argaty 20 Apr.Singles Tom Dubh, Callander 20 May and 24 Jun; Airthrey, BoA 7 Jun; Cocksburn Res, BoA 8 and 17 Jul; Lossburn Res, BoA 30 Sep and Polmaise Woods 15 Dec.

GREAT SPOTTED WOODPECKER *Dendrocopus major* (B, W)

F   1 Plean CP 31 Jan, 10 Apr and drumming there 10 May. Dunmore Woods, Airth: singles 20 Mar, 13 and 17 Jul, 14 Oct, 13 and 23 Nov. 1 Skinflats 16 Apr. Nested Strathavon Fm, Slamannan 5 Jun. 2 Carron Glen 17 Jun. 2 Skinflats 6 Oct. 1 Wallacestone, Falkirk 9 Nov.

C   Alva: singles Woodland Park 2 Feb, R Devon 6 May and 11 Sep. 1 Vicar's Br, E Dollar 25 Feb. Gartmorn: to E of site 21 Mar, 13, 14 (2 at dam) and 27 Apr. Tillicoultry: 2 at Tait Place 25 Mar with singles there throughout Jun and to NE of village 10 Dec. Single E of Clackmannan 28 Apr and 2 there 25 Nov. 1 W of Dollar 29 Apr and in the glen 20 May. 1 Menstrie 6 and 20 May and 1 along Menstrie-Alva old road 3 Jun. 1 Cambus 2 Oct and 18 Dec. Singles Castlebridge

Business Park, Forestmill 19, 20, 22 Nov and 12 Dec. 1 Blackgrange 10 Dec.

S   1 Cocksburn Res 2 Feb, 19 Sep with 2 there 29 Nov. Singles Callander 17 Feb and 20 Dec; Carron Valley Res 18 Feb, 24 Mar, 10 Nov with 2 there 20 Nov; Blairdrummond 21 Feb; L Rusky and 2 drumming L Menteith 8 Mar; Throsk 25 Mar; drumming L Lubnaig 27 Mar. In breeding season: singles L Tay, Killin 1 Apr; David Marshall Lodge, L Ard Forest 10 Apr; Brig o'Turk 15 Apr; Cobleland, Aberfoyle 21 Apr; L Achray and 2 at L Venachar 27 Apr; Aithrey, BoA 31 May; Lanrick 3 Jun; Sheriffmuir, E of Dunblane 17 Jul and Doune 21 Jul. Winter: 1 Dunblane, Allan Water 3 Sep with 2 S of village 6 Oct and 1 Kippenross 25 Oct. 2 Lossburn 30 Sep; 1 Drumbowie Res, Denny 1 Oct; 2 BoD, Argaty 31 Oct; Gargunnock 11 Nov and Gart, Callander 13 Dec.

SKYLARK   *Alauda arvensis*   (B, W)

The first singing birds were at Carse of Lecropt 17 Feb.

F   At least 2 still singing Westfield, Airth 11 Oct. 140 Skinflats 25 Oct.

C   Family party R Devon, Alva-Menstrie 18 Jul.

S   11 Carse of Lecropt 24 Nov with 30 there 11 Dec.

SAND MARTIN   *Riparia riparia* (B)

Arrival: 1 Gartmorn and R Devon, Menstrie 19 Mar was a day earlier than in 2006 and 2 days later than in 2005. This was followed by 5 at L Watston 31 Mar, 1 Lanrick 5 Apr and ca 10 Gart GP 8 Apr. Departure: the only report was of a single Kinneil 14 Sep, which was a day later than in 2006 and 21 days later than in 2005.

F   30$^+$ R Carron, Dunipace 18 May.

C   Ca. 110 Cambus Village Pool 16 Apr. 40 Blackdevon Wetlands 16 May. 21 AOT Glenfoot, R Devon 25 May.

S   152 nests in excavations Gart GP 17 Jun. 45 AOT R Teith, Lots of Callander 18 Jun.

SWALLOW   *Hirundo rustica* (B)

Spring arrival: 1 Stirling golf course 6 Mar was 25 days earlier than in 2006 and 28 days earlier than in 2005. This was followed by 1 Kersiepow, Alva 18 Mar with the next not until 10 Apr at Strathavon Fm, Slamannan; 4 BoD, Argaty 12 Apr; singles Skinflats, Ashfield and 4 Dunblane 14 Apr.

Autumn departure: 1 Blackdevon Wetlands 21 Sep; ca 15 Blaefaulds Denny 1 Oct; 1 Burn of Cambus 3 Oct and 6 Blackness 5 Oct, which was 11 days earlier than in 2006 and 28 days earlier than in 2005.

F   150 Skinflats 20 Jul. 90 Kinneil 14 Sep.

C   Nested Castlebridge Business Park, Forestmill (3 chicks) 13 Aug.

S   Nested Gatehouse, Polmaise (5 chicks) 30 Jul. 30 Doune 15 Sep. 53 Stirling 18 Sep. 12 Whitehill, Cowie 19 Sep.

HOUSE MARTIN   *Delichon urbica*   (B)

Arrival in Apr: 1 Stirling Br 9th was 5 days earlier than in 2006 and 2 days later than in 2005. This was followed by 4 Kinbuck 15th, 1 BoA 19th and 5 R Carron, Carronshore 20th.

Departure in Sep: 10 Stirling 2nd and 25 Flanders Moss 11th, which was 20 days earlier than in 2006 and 29 days earlier than in 2005.

F   2$^+$ nests N Doll, Airth 25 May.

C   1$^+$ nest Coalsnaughton.

S   4$^+$ prs bred Killin 12 May. 1$^+$ nest Museum Hall, BoA.

TREE PIPIT   *Anthus trivialis* (B)

Arrival in April: 1 E of Gartmorn 13th was 4 days earlier than in 2006 and 1 day later than in 2005. Then singles Aberfoyle 14th; Brig o'Turk, L Venachar and L Achray 15th; 2 BoD, Doune 20th; 6+ Gartmorn 28th, Flanders Moss 29th and Balhearty 30th.

F   3 Dunmore Moss, Airth 1 May with 1 there 25 May.

S   1 Old Drymen Road, L Ard Forest 26 May. 5 Lendrick Hill, Brig o'Turk 27 May. Ca 25 Coillie Coire Chuilc, Tyndrum18 Jun.

MEADOW PIPIT *Anthus pratensis* (B, W)

    Continues to be scarce mid-winter.

F   17 Skinflats 20 Jan with 20 there 14 Apr.

C   30 on newly excavated pool Blackdevon Wetlands 30 Oct.

S   15 Nether Carse 26 Feb. 55 in flock at Lynns, Sheriffmuir 5 Jul. 64 Auchinlay Rd, Dunblane 25 Aug. Stonehill 28 Aug. 14 Newton Crescent, Dunblane 22 Sep. 23 Gart GP 20 Dec.

ROCK PIPIT *Anthus petrosus* (w)

    At traditional sites along Falkirk shore.

F   2 Kincardine Br 16 Jan (DMB).

GREY WAGTAIL *Motacilla cinerea* (B, w)

F   1 Blackness 17 Feb with 2 there 5 Oct. 1 Skinflats 28 Aug.

C   Alva: singles in Glen 23 Jan, 7 Mar, 15 Apr (pr), 12 Nov; 2 in Woodland Park 9 Apr, at Balquharn 21 Jul. River Devon: singles Alva-Menstrie 2 and 18 Apr, 1 Oct, 16 Dec; 1 Cambus 24 Feb, 4 Apr, 10 Aug, 2 on 2 Oct; 2 Rumbling Br 1 Apr. Singles Tillicoultry Glen 12 May; Dollar Glen 20 May. 2 Gartmorn Dam 12 Sep. 1 W of Menstrie 17 Nov. 1 Cambus Pools 30 Dec.

S   1 Plean CP 31 Jan. Allan Water: 1 Dunblane 5 Feb, 5 Mar, 4 there 2 Aug, 1 on 10 Nov; BoA 1 on 6 Oct. 1 Cocksburn Res 21 Feb, 14 Mar, 2 there 15 Aug. 1 Stirling 19 Mar. 2 Benmore Glen 4 Apr. 2 L Ard Forest 10 Apr, 1 on 26 May. Singles L Katrine 15 Apr; Garrison, Inversnaid 5 May; Airthrey 17 May. 2 Carron Glen 17 Jun. Singles W of Cambusbarron and S of Kippen 7 Jul; Lossburn 31 Jul. 2 R Teith, Lecropt 18 Sep, 1 on 11 Dec.

PIED WAGTAIL *Motacilla alba* (B, w)

    More records from the first winter season, possibly as a result of more intense recording, but not from the second winter season: 9 Jan records (4 in 2005, 3 in 2006), including 6 Blackdevon Wetlands 16 Jan, 22 feeding Carse of Lecropt 23 Jan, 4 Skinflats. 11 Feb records (1 in 2005, 6 in 2006), including 4 Skinflats 23 Feb. Only 6 Nov records (as in 2005 and 2006): singles Blackdevon Wetlands 5th; Powbridge Fm and Westfield Fm, Airth 13th; Forth, Nether Carse 26th; R Devon, Alva 29th and 2 Stirling University 29th. Seven Dec records (as in 2005 and 2006): 1 Stirling University 3rd and 2 on 13th; Alloa tip 15th; Gartmorn 18th; Lower Auchinlay Fm, Dunblane 27th and Forth, Nether Carse 31st.

F   35 Strathavon Fm, Slamannan 13 Aug. White Wagtails (M.a.alba): 2 Skinflats 31 Mar, 6 there 14 Apr, 14 on 20th, 5 on 22nd and 8 on 24th; 1 Cambus Village Pool 18 Apr with 2 there 8 May.

C   6 Blackdevon Wetlands 5 Mar with 4 there on 20th. 30 King's Park, Stirling 12 Mar. 8 Gartmorn 14 Mar.

S   Pr bred BoD, wind farm. 2 prs bred Kipenross, Dunblane. 111 King's Park, Stirling 21 Sep with 56 there 3 Oct.

WAXWING *Bombycilla garrulus* (w)

F   1 St. Ninians 10 Dec (BRG).

S   2 Airthrey 27 and 28 Mar with 1 there 29th (ACC, CJP).

DIPPER *Cinclus cinclus* (B, W)

F   1 R Carron, Carron Works 13 Nov.

C   R Devon: 2 at Alva 7 Jan, 2 including 1 in song at Tait's Tomb, Tillicoultry 25 Nov. 1 Woodland Park, Alva 15 Jan. 1 Tillicoultry Glen 12 May.

S   1 Doune Castle 16 Mar. 1 Aberfoyle and 2 Strathfillan, Tyndrum 14 Apr. 1 L Tay, Killin 28 Apr. 2 Allan Water, Dunblane 8 May with 1 on 10 Nov. 1 Inverlocharig

9 May. 2 Todholes, Fintry Hills 15 May. Bred BoD, Ardoch Burn and present all year BoD, Garvald Burn. 1 R Teith, Inverardoch 15 Sep. 1 close to summit of Ben Chabair (800m asl). 1 L Voil 18 Nov.

WREN *Troglodytes troglodytes* (B, W)

    Widespread and common. Under-recorded.

C   Family party R Devon, Alva-Menstrie 6 Jun. 9 Woodland Park, Alva 20 Sep.

S   1 singing Coneyhill, BoA 17 Feb. 14 King's Park, Stirling 2 Apr. Pr bred (br4) BoD, windfarm. 8 Airthrey 20 Nov.

DUNNOCK *Accentor modularis* (B, W)

    Widespread and common. Under-recorded.

C   6 Woodland Park, Alva 9 Apr. 6 Gartmorn Dam 14 May.

S   8 King's Park, Stirling 2 Mar. Ad feeding 2 Y Dunblane 12 May.

ROBIN *Erithacus rubecula* (B,W)

    Under-recorded.

F   15 King's Park, Stirling 27 Apr.

C   11 Woodland Park, Alva 2 Mar. 14 Gartmorn 12 Sep.

S   1 singing Coneyhill, BoA from 22 Jan had a newly fledged bird on 16 Jun.

REDSTART *Phoenicurus phoenicurus* (B)

    Arrival in Apr: 1 L Tay, Killin 22nd was 1 day earlier than in 2006 and 3 days later than in 2005. This was followed by 2 at L Venachar, Brig o'Turk and L Achray on 27th (JPH, AM).

S   M L Ard (E end) 3 May. 1 nr Stronachlachar and 2 BoD, Doune Lodge 5 May. 1 Lake of Menteith 9 Jul (DT, DAC, DOE, JT).

WHINCHAT *Saxicola rubetra* (B)

    Spring arrival in April has been remarkably consistent over the last five years. 1 Flanders Moss 27th was 2-4 days earlier than during 2003-2006. This was followed by a M in song G Dubh, L Ard Forest 28th and 3 AOT Flanders Moss 29th.

    Autumn departure: M Pow Burn, W of Airth 8 Aug was 24 days earlier than in 2006.

C   1 West Loaningbank, Menstrie 20 May.

S   2 M BoD, Doune Lodge 8 May with 3 at Argaty 19 May and pr (br3) bred at the wind farm. Singles Cocksburn Res and Inverlochlarig 9 May.

STONECHAT *Saxicola torquata* (b, w)

F   Kinneil: 2 in Jan, 1in Oct, 2 in Nov and Dec. Skinflats: 2 in Jan, 1 in Feb, 2 in Oct and Dec. 1 S Alloa 16 Jan. 2 Powfoulis Manor 25 Oct. M Powbridge, Airth 13 Nov. 2 Gilston, Falkirk 11 Dec. M Higgins Neuk 18 Dec.

C   Blackdevon Wetlands: 2 in Jan, 3 in Feb, 2 in Mar, 1 in Oct, 3 in Nov and 2 in Dec. Tullibody: 2 in Feb, pr with 3 Y Jun, 2 in Sep. R Devon, Alva: 2 in Feb and Sep. 1 E Coalsnaughton 27 Apr. 2 SW of Alva 30 Apr and 11 May.

S   2 Polmaise lagoons in Jan, Mar, May, Aug, pr and 2 juvs in Sep, 2 in Oct, Nov and Dec. 4 Flanders Moss 31 Mar, pr 29 Apr, 12 prs 12 May, 3 in 2 Dec. F Harperstone 31 Mar, M 27 Apr, M and juv 1 Jun. During breeding season reported from Gargunnock Hills (pr); Strathfillan; L Chon; Sheriffmuir where also 2 on 29 Nov; Garrison, Inversnaid (2); by Stronachlachar; Gleann Breac-nic (2); Inverlochlarig; L Arklet (2); BoD, Drumloist (pr); Carron Valley Res where also 2 in Nov; Tom Dubh, Callander; Cocksburn where 7 on 14 Nov. 6 Lerrocks, Argaty 27 Sep. Malling, 3 L of Menteith 28 Sep.

WHEATEAR *Oenanthe oenanthe* (B)

    Spring arrival: 1 Glen Finglas 25 Mar was 9 days earlier than in 2006 and 4 days later than in 2005. Then in Apr 6 Strathfillan, Tyndrum and 1 Skinflats 14th; 10 Strathavon Fm, Slamannan 25th and 12 on 1st May; BoD, Bows 27th April.

Autumn departure: 1 Auchinlay Rd, Dunblane 8 Sep; 2 Glenhead 22 Sep; 2 Skinflats 7 Oct and BoD, wind farm 9 Oct, which was 4 days earlier than in 2006 and 35 days later than in 2005.

F   2 Glenhead 19 Aug.1 Skinflats 22 Aug.

C   1 West Loaningbank, Menstrie 20 May.

S   1 Flanders Moss 1 May. 2 Harperstone 3 Aug.

BLACKBIRD *Turdus merula* (B, W)

F   25 Skinflats 27 Jan with 15 there 23 Feb.

C   14 R Devon, Alva 7 Jan with 16 there 16 Dec. 12 Gartmorn 27 Jun.

S   15 Airthrey 3 Jan and 11 Dec. M in sub-song Coneyhill, BoA 11 Jan. 28 King's Park, Stirling 21 Jan with 15 on 13 Feb, 27 on 2 Mar, 24 on 27 Apr, 32 on 16 May, 24 on 7 Jun, 12 on 13 Jul, 15 on 18 Oct and 21 on 20 Nov. 25 Blair Drummond 19 Dec. 12 Drip Moss 30 Dec.

FIELDFARE *Turdus pilaris* (W)

Spring departure in Mar: 50 Argaty and 13 Forth, Nether Carse 23rd, then 75 Fishcross 27th, which was 48 days earlier than in 2006 and 33 days earlier than in 2005.

Autumn arrival in October: 2 Argaty 7th was 20 days earlier than in 2006 and 13 days earlier than in 2005. This was followed by 130 by Flanders Moss, 500 Callander and ca 500 Strathavon Fm, Slamannan 18th; mixed thrush flock of 300 Auchenbowie 23rd; 140 Gilston, Falkirk 24th; 5 Forth, Nether Carse and 150 Skinflats 25th and 156 (7 flocks) >SW Ashfield 27th.

F   350 Airth 20 Jan. 140 Powfoulis 21 Jan. 140 Gilston, Falkirk 24 Oct. 150 Skinflats 25 Oct with 60 there 11 Nov.

C   280 Kennetpans 5 Jan. 60 R Devon, Alva-Menstrie 7 Nov. 66 E of Clackmannan 9 Nov. 150 Blackdevon Wetlands 15 Dec.

S   80 Wester Boreland, Thornhill 5 Jan. 270 Carron Br, Townfoot 16 Jan. 148 Lerrocks, Argaty 23 Jan with ca 200 there 13 Feb. 80 Plean Castle >SW and 140 Stonehill 2 Nov. 75 Lecropt 7 Dec was the largest flock from this site which traditionally held much larger flocks. 78 Forth, Nether Carse 31 Dec.

SONG THRUSH *Turdus philomelos* (B, W)

Under-recorded.

More winter records (singles or twos) than in past. Jan: recorded from Kinneil, Cambus; Gartmorn; R Devon, Menstrie-Alva; Stirling, BoA and Dunblane. Feb: Cambus; R Devon, Menstrie-Alva; Blackdevon Wetlands: Tullibody; W of Alva; BoA. In Dec: Carse of Lecropt; The Meadows, Callander.

C   5 Gartmorn 14 May.

REDWING *Turdus iliacus* (W)

Spring departure: 6 Union Canal 6 Mar was followed by ca 170 L. Rusky 8 Mar, which was 3 days later than in 2006 and 5 days earlier than in 2005.

Autumn arrival in Sep: 28 Lerrocks, Argaty >SW and 2 Newton Crescent, Dunblane 27th were 14 days earlier than in 2006 and 11 days earlier than in 2005. Then ca 30 Strathavon Fm, Slamannan, 47 Ashfield and ca 50 L Rusky 28th; 15 Doune 29th. In Oct: 50+ Kippenross, Dunblane and 30 R Devon, Alva-Menstrie 1st;12 Skinflats 6th; 10 Dunblane 7th and 12 King's Park, Stirling 12th.

F   60 Skinflats 25 Oct.

S   Ca 200 Carse of Lecropt 14 Jan with 60 there 26 Jan. 70 Lerrocks, Argaty 23 Jan with 62 there 13 Dec. 312 Drip Moss and 223 Blairdrummond 23 Jan with 120 in latter location 7 Feb.

MISTLE THRUSH *Turdus viscivorus* (B, W)

Under-recorded.

F   25+ Dunmore Tower and 8 Skinflats 14 Oct.

S   8 Ledcharrie, G Dochart 24 Jan. Singing Viewforth, Stirling 25 Jan. 12 Lone Shieling, L Rusky 28 Sep. 35 Wester Cambushinnie, Kinbuck 21 Sep. 15 Airthrey 22 Oct.

GRASSHOPPER WARBLER *Locustella naevia* (b)

Spring arrival in Apr: 1 R Devon, Alva-Menstrie 25th was 2 days earlier than in 2006 and 2 days later than in 2005. Then singles Skinflats; R Carron, Carronshore and Darnrig Moss 26th; L Tay, Killin and Flanders Moss 27th; 3 Westfield, Airth 30th.

F   1 Skinflats 12, 13, 18 May and 21 Jul.

S   2 Flanders Moss 1 May and 30 Jun. 1 L Arklet 5 May. 1 nr Haugh, W of Dollar 26 May.

SEDGE WARBLER *Acrocephalus schoenobaenus* (B)

Spring arrival: 1 Skinflats 25 Apr was 2 days earlier than in 2006 and 6 days earlier than in 2005. Then 4 on 0.5 mile of R Devon, Alva-Menstrie 30 Apr. 2 Kinneil and 1 Menstrie 4 May and 3 Drip Carse 5 May.

Autumn departure: 2 Shieldhill, Falkirk 10 Aug were 4 days earlier than in 2006 and 27 days earlier than in 2005.

F   3 Skinflats 11 and 12 May and 2 there 7 Jul.

C   In May: Gartmorn, Blackgrange (5), Tullibody Inch (11). Ad feeding 2 Y R Devon, Alva-Menstrie 8 Aug.

S   3 Ashfield 3 Jun. Ad feeding 2 Y Polmaise lagoons 30 Jul.

WHITETHROAT *Sylvia communis* (B)

Spring arrival: 1 Skinflats 23 Apr was 3 days earlier than in 2006 and 7 days earlier than in 2005. Then 1 Old Railway, Menstrie 25th; 1 Cambus Village Pool 26th; 2 Dunmore, 1 E of Gartmorn and 1 R Carron, Carronshore 27th; 3 Blairdrummond Moss and 1 Dunblane 30th.

Autumn departure: 2 Skinflats 2 Aug were 21 days earlier than in 2006 and 36 days earlier than in 2005.

F   3 Skinflats 11 May. 3 Kinneil 4 May.

C   3 Muckhart 26 May. 4 Blackgrange 30 Jun.

S   1 Lanrick 8 May. 1 Kinbuck Br 31 May. 1 Ashfield 3 Jun.

GARDEN WARBLER *Sylvia borin* (B)

Spring arrival: 1 S of Forestmill 28 Apr was 6 days earlier than in 2006 and 4 days earlier than in 2005. Then 3 Blairdrummond Moss and Westfield, Dunmore Woods 30 Apr. 1 Drip Carse 5 May. 1 Muckhart 7 May. 2 Allan Water, Dunblane and 1 Argaty 8 May. 1 Dunblane 9 May.

F   1 singing R Carron, Dunipace 18 May.

C   9 Gartmorn 14 May. 1 Alva Glen 3 Jun. 1 Old Railway, Menstrie 11 Jun. 1 Blackgrange 30 Jun. Family party R Devon Alva-Menstrie 18 Jul.

S   5 Lower G Lochay 12 May. 2 singing Blairdrummond 13 May. 1 Lanrick 3 Jun.

BLACKCAP *Sylvia atricapilla* (B)

Winter records: F Springwood Ave, Stirling 1 Jan and M there 13 Jan. M Dunblane 6 and 7 Jan. M and F Alexander Dr, BoA 28 Jan. 1 Doune 12 Feb. 1 Blackness 5 Oct. 1 BoA 30 Oct. F 19 to 28 Dec Springwood Av, Stirling and M there 20 Dec.

Spring arrival in Apr: 1 BoA 25 Mar and 1 Airthrey 29 Apr could have been overwintering birds. In April: 1 E of Gartmorn 13th were 7 days later than in 2006 and 3 days later than in 2005. Then 4 Dunblane 14th; 1 Coneyhill BoA and Skinflats 21st; 3 Blairdrummond Moss 30th.

F   Singing Carron House, Carronshore 5 May and R Carron, Dunipace 18 May.

C   2 Dollar Glen feeding Y 20 May. Pr with nest material Tullibody 26 Jun.

S   Males BoD, Argaty and Doune Lodge 8 May. 3 singing Plean CP 10 May.

WOOD WARBLER *Phylloscopus sibilatrix* (B)
　　Under-recorded.
　　Spring arrival: 3 L Venachar 27 Apr were 2 days earlier than in 2006 and 3 days
　　earlier than in 2005. Then 1 Mine Wood, BoA 30 Apr. 2 Glen Road, Dunblane
　　and 2 Pass of Leny 3 May. 4 Lower G Lochay 12 May. 1 L Tay, Killin 13 May.
C　　1 singing Dollar Glen 20 May.
S　　5 singing Brig o'Turk 27 May. 2 Cocksburn Res 6 Jun. 2 singing BoD, Bracklinn
　　24 Jun.
CHIFFCHAFF *Phylloscopus collybita* (B)
　　Spring arrival: 1 Airthrey 15 Mar was 16 days earlier than in 2006 and 9 days
　　earlier than in 2005. Then 1 R Devon, Alva Menstrie 20th ; 2 Larbert 26th; 5
　　Gartmorn, 1 L Watston and 1 BoD, Lundie 31st.
　　Autumn departure: 1 Skinflats 6 Oct was 2 days later than in 2006 and 10 days
　　later than in 2005.
F　　Breeding season: old Falkirk tunnel, Union Canal; Dollar Park and Calendar
　　Park, Falkirk.
C　　Breeding season: West Loaningbank and Bluebell Wood, Menstrie; Alva Glen.
S　　Breeding season: Allan Water, Dunblane; Plean CP (2); Bannockburn; Airthrey;
　　Coneyhill, BoA; Cocksburn Res (2); Viewforth, King's Park (4) and Royal
　　Infirmary, Stirling; Coneyhill, BoA; L Venachar (2).
WILLOW WARBLER *Phylloscopus trochilus* (B)
　　Spring arrival in Apr: 1 Cambus Village Pool 11th was 3 days earlier than in
　　2006 and 8 days later than in 2005. Then singles E of Gartmorn, Kippenross
　　and Dunblane and Argaty 13th; 5 Skinflats 14th after which widespread.
　　Autumn departure: 3 Gartmorn 12 Sep and 1 Blackness 5 Oct, which was 18
　　days later than in 2006 and 1 day earlier than in 2005.
F　　7+ Kinneil 7 Aug.
C　　13 Gartmorn 16 Apr with 23there 14 May and 25 on 7 Aug. 7 Muckhart 7 May.
　　Pr and 3 Y R Devon, Alva-Menstrie 18 Jul.
S　　5 King's Park, Stirling 19 Apr with 8 there 27 Apr. 5 Brig o'Turk 27 Apr. 8
　　Blackgrange 20 May. 11 Cocksburn Res 23 May. 6 Old Drymen Rd, L Ard Forest
　　26 May.
GOLDCREST *Regulus regulus* (B, W)
　　Under-recorded. No notable records were received.
SPOTTED FLYCATCHER *Muscicapa striata* (B)
　　Spring arrival in May: 1 Gartmorn 19th was 10 days later than in 2006 and 5
　　days later than in 2005. Then 1 Dollar G 20th; 2 Blairdrummond Moss 22nd.
　　Autumn departure: 1 Skinflats 24 Aug was 8 days later than in 2006.
C　　Pr visiting tree nest hole 31 May. 1 E of Gartmorn 5 Jun.
S　　During breeding season: singles Lanrick 3 Jun; Airthrey 7th; Baxter's Loan,
　　Dunblane 10th; Arnprior and Lake of Menteith, 2 R Forth, Cardross Br and 3
　　Coillie Coire Chuilc, Tyndrum all 17th. 1 S of Kippen 7 Jul; 1 G Lochay 10th. 1
　　Glenis Rd, Stirling 7 Jul. Pr and 2 juvs Lossburn 31 Jul.
PIED FLYCATCHER *Ficedula hypoleuca* (b)
S　　3 M Lower G Lochay 12 May (DT).
LONG-TAILED TIT *Aegithalos caudatus* (B, W)
F　　15 Skinflats 27 Jan and 12 Sep.
C　　16 Blackgrange 20 May. 15 R Devon, Alva-Menstrie 23 Oct.
S　　15 Airthrey 11 Jan. 15 Plean CP 31 Jan. 3 juvs Blairlogie 8 Jun. 17 L Dochart 28 Oct.
COAL TIT *Periparus ater* (B, W)
　　Widespread but under-recorded.
S　　Singing Coneyhill, BoA 4, 5 and 7 Jan. Ad feeding 2 juvs Dunblane garden 1 Jun.

BLUE TIT *Cyanistes caeruleus* (B, W)
Under-recorded.
C   Alva: 16 R Devon, 7 Jan and 16 Woodland Park 22 Jan. 15 Gartmorn 6 Feb. 15 Blackgrange 18 Feb.
S   1 singing Airthrey 15 Feb. 15 King's Park, Stirling 8 Apr. 16 Blairdrummond Moss 19 Dec.
GREAT TIT *Parus major* (B, W)
Under-recorded.
F   15 Skinflats 27 Jan.
C   16 Woodland Park, Alva 2 Mar.
S   Singing Coneyhill, BoA 4 Jan; Callander and L Venachar 11 Feb.
TREECREEPER *Certhia familiaris* (B, W)
Under-recorded
F   Breeding season: 1 Bonnybridge 9 May. Winter: 3 Polmaise Wood 8 Dec.
C   Breeding season: Menstrie; E of Clackmannan; E of Gartmorn; Alva, Woodland Park and Balquharn.
S   Breeding season: Airthrey (4); Aberfoyle; Brig o'Turk; Kelty Water; L Venachar; Old Drymen Rd, L Ard Forest.
*GREAT GREY SHRIKE *Lanius excubitor*
C   1 Menstrie Glen 15 Dec (JRC).
S   1 Carron Valley Res 12 Mar (DAC).
Correction from 2006: due to an error during data compilation, the record of 2 birds at Skinflats 23 Sep (RS) should be annulled. The above two records therefore become the 20th and 21st records, respectively, for the recording area.
JAY *Garrulus glandarius* (B, W)
F   1 Larbert 6 Jul.1 Dunmore Woods 14 Oct. 2 Denny 14 Nov.
C   4 Tullibody East 20 Apr. 2 E of Clackmannan 28 Apr and 9 Nov. 1 Dollar Glen 20 May. 1 Tait Place, Tillicoultry 11 Jun. 1 dead on B9140 at Brandyhill Wood, Fishcross. 1 R Devon, Alva-Menstrie 1 Oct. 2 calling Castlebridge Business Park, Forestmill 7 Nov. 1 Gartmorn 26 Nov. 1 NE of Tillicoultry 10 Dec.
S   Jan-Feb: 2 Pendreich, BoA. Singles Plean CP; Park of Keir, Dunblane; Argaty; Balquhidder, Strathyre; L Tay, Killin. Breeding season: 1 Tom Dubh, Callander 20 May and 24 Jun. 1 Old Drymen Rd, L Ard Forest 26 May. Aug: 1 Cocksburn. Sep: Carron Valley Res (also 2 Nov), Dunmore Moss (2^{+} also Nov), Airthrey (also Oct), L Rusky (also Oct), L Voil. Oct: N of BoA (also Nov); Cobleland, Aberfoyle. Nov: Flanders Moss; Darn Walk, Dunblane; Strathyre (2). Dec: 2 Plean CP; 2 Cocksburn; 2 Gillie's Hill, Stirling; Hill o'Row; 1 Gart GP.
MAGPIE *Pica pica* (B, W)
Continues to be very scarce NW of Dunblane. Abundant around Stirling but is not usually as frequent in the west; large groups now widespread in Falkirk
F   15 Fallin 6 Feb. 14 Union Canal 6 Mar. 11 Haircraigs 28 Mar.
C   11 Tullibody N 24 Jan.
S   15 Airthrey 12 Jan was a low count compared to past roost counts there. 10 Buchany, Milton of Cambus 28 Jan. 2 Tom Dubh, Callander 20 May with 1 there 24 Jun.
JACKDAW *Corvus monedula* (B, W)
Under-recorded.
S   Roost flights over Coneyhill, BoA: 90 on 15 Jan, 162 on 29 Jan, 188 on 28 Feb.
ROOK *Corvus frugilegus* (B, W)
Systematic counts of known rookeries (e.g. BoA, Gartmorn, Forth and Clyde Canal, Lake of Menteith, etc.) needed.
F   Active rookery at The Pineapple-Airth Apr-Jun (no count).

S   300 Greenyards Fm, Dunblane 11 Nov. Large pre-roost gathering Plean 27 Nov. Major roost flight over Coneyhill, BoA (prob Rooks and Jackdaws) noted in Jan, 12 Feb, 28 Sep and 14 Oct.

CARRION CROW *Corvus corone* (B, W)

F   48 Skinflats 18 Feb with 26 there 23 Sep.

S   37 King's Park, Stirling 13 Feb.

HOODED CROW *Corvus cornix* (b, w)

F   1 Union Canal 14 Jul.

C   1 R Devon, Alva 21 Jul.

S   2 G Dochart 24 Jan (also 5 hybrids there) with 11 there 28 Oct. 7 Strathfillan, Tyndrum 14 Apr with 2 Tyndrum 17 Apr. 1 Balquhidder 9 May. 2 G Lochay 6 Jun with 4 there 10 Jul. 1 Clash Fm, Callander 18 Jun. 1 L Voil 28 Oct.

RAVEN *Corvus corax* (B, W)

      There were again a number of reports from south/southwest of the core Callander-Doune-Dunblane area.

F   2 > N Carron 22 Sep. 1 > NW Skinflats 23 Nov.

C   3 Dollar Glen 1 May with 2 repeatedly in quarry there 20 May. 1 over Castlebridge Business Park, Forestmill 28 Mar and 7 May. 1 Tillicoultry Glen 12 May. 8 NE of Tillicoultry 10 Dec.

S   From core area: 1 Chip Dhuibh, Menteith Hills 1 Feb. 1 Stuc a Chroin 6 Feb. 50 roosted BoD, Doune Lodge 6 Apr and 80 there 30 Dec. Pr fledged 3 Y BoD, Drumloist 9 Apr and b5 at Argaty. 2 Tom Dubh, Callander 20 May and 1 there 24 Jun. 16 BoD 3 Oct. 2 Ben A'an, Trossachs 3 Nov. 1 Cambusmore 23 Nov. 2 L Mahaick 20 Dec. Outside of core area: 3 Carron Valley Res 23 Jan with singles there over res, at Cringate and at Gartcarron 24 Mar, 1 at res 25 Mar and 2 there 10 Nov. 1 Flanders Moss 31 Jan and 2 there 2 Sep. 1 Dumyat 5 Feb. 1 Blairdrummond Moss 30 Apr. 1 Cocksburn 22 Aug. 2 Thornhill 29 Dec.

STARLING *Sturnus vulgaris* (B, W)

      Greatly under-reported.

F   2500 Orchardhead, Skinflats 10 Nov.

C   100 Coalsnaughton 15 Jun.

S   2200 Haugh Cottage, Forth in pre-roost flight over mouth of Bannock Burn 5 Nov.

HOUSE SPARROW *Passer domesticus* (B, W)

      Under-recorded.

F   Breeding season: Union Canal (22), Denny and Drumbowie. Non-breeding: 45 Stonehouse Fm, Skinflats 15 Sep.

C   Breeding season: 2 at Alva Glen 15 Apr.

S   Breeding season: Stirling Br, Riverside and Causewayhead, Stirling (14); Dunblane where ad fed 2 Y; Aberfoyle; L Ard Forest, Old Drymen Road. Non-breeding: 52 Kinbuck 4 Aug. 14 Blairdrummond Carse 19 Dec.

TREE SPARROW *Passer montanus* (B, W)

      Species again more widespread than in preceding years.

F   1-4 Skinflats 1 Feb and 1 Apr (by cottages), 25 May (Howkerse), with 11 on 6 Oct, 5 on 25 Oct (Orchardhead), 12 on 13 Nov (Brackenlees Fm), 9 on 20 Nov and 18 on 22 Nov. Outside breeding season also 1-2: Fallin, Blackness and Powfoulis Manor. 2-8 throughout year Kendieshill Fm, Maddiston.

C   Breeding season: R Devon, Alva; NE of Gartmorn; E of Clackmannan. Outside breeding season 1-3 birds: Jan to Mar: Westhaugh, Alva; Gartmorn and Kennetpans. Nov to Dec: E of Clackmannan (5) and Cambus.

S   16 Plean garden 21 Jan. 10 Thornhill Carse feeding station 8 Mar. 4 Carbrook Mains, Plean 7 May and 6 there 27 Jun. 10 (including pr with 6 Y) BoA 20 Jun. 8

Lecropt 18 Sep with 20 there at Netherton 9 Oct and 4 on 11 Dec. Ca 10 nr Hillhead SE of Cowie 19 Sep. 6 Forth, Nether Carse 26 Nov.
Addition from 2006: 60$^+$ Carse of Lecropt 20 Jul.

CHAFFINCH *Fringilla coelebs* (B, W)
S   Singing Coneyhill, BoA 7 Feb. 260 Lerrocks, Argaty 23 Feb and 300 there 13 Dec. 122 Blairdrummond Moss 19 Dec.

BRAMBLING *Fringilla montifringilla* (W)
F   34 Wester Jawcraig, Slamannan 7 Jan (RS). 2 Strathavon Fm, Slamannan 23 Oct (TF).
S   1 L Venachar 16 Jan (BRG). 1 Kinbuck 27 Oct (MVB).
Addition from 2006: 10$^+$ Muckhart 25 Nov.

GREENFINCH *Carduelis chloris* (B, W)
        Under-recorded.
S   20 Lerrocks, Argaty 23 Jan. 22 King's Park, Stirling 14 Feb. Pr feeding 3 juvs Dunblane garden 29 Jun. 80 Kinbuck 15 Dec. 42 Blairdrummond Carse 19 Dec.

GOLDFINCH *Carduelis carduelis* (B, W)
        No significant flocks reported from the Doune-Dunblane area.
F   18 Skinflats 25 Aug with 35 there 12 Sep and 75 on 15 Sep. 26 Kinneil 5 Sep, 40 there 4 Sep. 40 Airth 24 Dec.
C   40 R Devon, Alva-Menstrie 18 Jul included juvs.
S   Flocks of 9 and 11 Springwood Ave, Stirling daily in Jan. 10 L Ruskie 26 Jan. Ad fed 3 juvs Dunblane garden 12 Jun. 50 Doune 15 Sep.

SISKIN *Carduelis spinus* (B, W)
F   Mixed flock of 40-50 Siskins and Lesser Redpolls Darnrigg Moss, Slamannan 2 Nov.
C   M fed juv Dollar Glen 20 May.
S   35 Lerrocks, Argaty 23 Jan, 37 there 13 Dec. 30 L Ruskie 26 Jan. Ca 35 Chip Dhuibh, Menteith Hills1 Feb. Dunblane: 55 Newton Crescent 11 Feb, 88 on 25 Feb; 75 in a garden 25 Feb and 32 there 11 Mar. Flock Stirling garden Jan-Mar peaked at 23 on 22 Feb. 25 L of Menteith 25 Feb. 23 King's Park, Stirling 18 Sep. 36 Airthrey 1 Nov. 42 Craigenhall, Hill o'Row 24 Nov. 32 Cocksburn 2 Dec. 91 Wetherlaw Wood, Stirling 15 Dec.

LINNET *Carduelis cannabina* (B, W)
        Only small flock were in the Doune and Dunblane areas. No reports from the Carse of Lecropt.
F   260 Skinflats 21 Jan with 115 in fields there and 250 on saltmarsh 25 Oct. 170 S Alloa 22 Mar.
C   250 R Devon, Alva-Menstrie with 80 there 23 Oct; 50 S of Menstrie 1 Feb. 20 on newly excavated pool at Blackdevon Wetlands 10 Apr. 200 Glenochil prison 27 Jun was large flock at unusual time. 35 Gartmorn 26 Nov.
S   70 Kippenrait, Dunblane 11 Feb. 7 BoD 7 Apr with 5 at Waterside there 26 Jun and M and 3 juvs 5 Jul.

TWITE *Carduelis flavirostris* (b, W)
F   10 Kinneil 2 Jan with 3 there 25 Jan. 25 on saltmarsh at Powfoulis Manor 21 Jan with 14 there 25 Oct. 3 S Alloa 22 Mar. 80 on saltmarsh at Skinflats 25 Oct. 250 Airth 23 Dec.
C   2 Cambus 19 Mar. 120 Blackdevon Wetland 25 Nov.
S   1 L Venachar 18 Jan. 2 Benmore G 4 Apr. 2 BoD, Lodge 6 Apr. 3 G Finglas 27 May. Pr and b3 BoD, Uamh Beg 5 Jul and 1 heard there 23 Oct. 15 BoD, Argaty 17 Sep. 4 Lerrocks, Argaty and 42 Kippenrait, Dunblane 13 Dec.

LESSER REDPOLL *Carduelis cabaret* (b, W)
S   15 Dunblane garden 7 Jan. 4 Cromlix 8 Apr. 10 BoD, Drumloist 22 Apr with 6 at

Argaty 28 Apr. 18 Newton Crescent, Dunblane 21 Sep. 15 Craigenhall, Hill o'Row 24 Nov.

COMMON CROSSBILL *Loxia curvirostra* (b, W)

C   Pr Hillfoot Hill, Dollar 11 Feb (DT).

S   5 LVenachar 16 Jan. 3 L Ruskie 23 Jan (BRG, RAB). 1 singing Lerrocks, Argaty 22 Mar with 8 there 21 Apr, 8 on 22 Sep and 1 on 13 Dec. 7 N slopes Ben More 4 Apr. 8 BoD, Drumloist 9 Apr with 6 there 23 Jun. 4 Carron Valley Res 25 Mar with M there 26 Apr, 5 on 13 Jun and M andF 20 Nov (GO, MVB, JT, DOE, DAC, DMB). Pr Stronachlachar 5 May. 3 L Ard 2 May. Pr Gart GP 15 May. 8 Old Drymen Rd, L Ard Forest 26 May (DAC, DOE, DT, LMB). 3 over Cardross Br, R Forth 17 Jun. 2 Coillie Coire Chuilc, Tyndrum 19 Jun. 2 -> BoA 27 Jun (JT, DMB). 1 Hermitage Wood, Airthrey 17 Nov. 5 Hutchinson Pond, Cromlix 18 Nov. 10 Doune 2 Dec. 20 Wetherlaw Wood, Stirling 15 Dec. 14 Cairnoch Hill Wood and 15 Touchadam Muir 16 Dec. 18 BoD, Lodge 30 Dec (CJP, DOE).

Addition from 2006: pr (M singing) Gart GP 18 Mar with 6 there 25 Jul. 9 Nether Moss, S of Muckhart 25 Nov (DT)

BULLFINCH *Pyrrhula pyrrhula* (B, W)

F   8 Dunmore 11 Feb. 16 Darnrigg Moss, Slamannan 24 Jan and 7 there 2 Nov. 1 Dorrator Br, R Carron 30 May.

C   M and 3 Y NE Tullibody 27 Jun. 5 Gartmorn 18 Dec.

S   22 King's Park, Stirling 23 Jan. 6 Airthrey 23 Jan, 2 Apr and 13 Dec. 6 Springwood Ave, Stirling 31 Jan. 9 Lerrocks, Argaty 23 Feb. M and 2 newly fledged juvs Coneyhill, BoA 23 Jun. 6 Argaty 1 Dec. 19 Touchadam 16 Dec. 17 BoD, Doune Lodge 30 Dec.

SNOW BUNTING *Plectrophenax nivalis* (W)

C   3 King's Seat, Ochils 18 Nov. 45 Menstrie Glen 16 Dec (KB, JRC).

S   1 Ben More summit 1 Apr. 2 BoD, Uamh Mhor 23 Nov with 8 there 29 Nov. (JT, KD). 28 Cringate Muir 16 Dec (CJP).

Addition from 2005: 100 BoD, Uamh Mhor 7 Dec and 50 there 27 Dec (KD).

YELLOWHAMMER *Emberiza citrinella* (B, W)

F   Skinflats: 20 on 26 Jan, 26 on 18 Feb, 3 on 22 Apr and 24 on 29 Dec.

C   25 Gartmorn 28 Jan. 85 Rhind, Tullibody Inch 4 Feb. Breeding season: Menstrie and R Devon, Alva.

S   48 Lerrocks, Argaty 23 Jan. Ca 30 Blairdrummond Carse 1 Feb with 53 there 19 Dec. During breeding season: Callander; R Forth, Cardross Br and Carse of Lecropt. 40[+] Carse of Lecropt 20 Nov.

REED BUNTING *Emberiza schoeniclus* (B, W)

F   Skinflats: 50 on 20 Jan, 2 flocks of 28 each on pools and saltmarsh 18 Feb, 15 on 23 Feb and 3 at pond 3 May. Kinneil: 11 on 25 Jan, 6 on 2 Feb and 12 on 19 Oct. M in Grangemouth garden 17 Apr. 1 Haircraigs 22 May.

C   29 Westhaugh, Alva 19 Jan. 5 Blackgrange 21 Jan. 5 R Devon, Alva 4 Mar. During breeding season: newly excavated pool, Blackdevon Wetlands 4 and 9 May; Tullibody Inch (6); Woodland Park, Alva; R Forth, Cambus to Inches (10) and Gartmorn (4). 7[+] at roost Castlebridge Business Park, Forestmill 7 Nov.

S   28 Rossburn Lane, Drip Moss 23 Jan. Breeding season: Airthrey; R Forth, Cardross Br; Flanders Moss (4M) and L Tay, Killin. 8 Cocksburn Res 24 Oct. 8 Sheriffmuir 29 Nov.

ESCAPED SPECIES

SWAN (CHINESE) GOOSE *Anser cygnoides*

This is the first time this species has been reported from our recording area.

S   3 Airthrey 17 Nov (CJP). This is likely to include the same bird present there since at least 2003.

COCKATIEL *Nymphicus hollandicus*

This is the second record of this species for our recording area.

C   1 of the grey or cinnamon colour mutation Cambus Pool 13 May had damage to tail (AET).

'COME NORTH': GLASSERT GAME BOOKS AND DIARIES

Alastair Durie and Karl Magee

Through the kindness of the Joynson family, the archives department of the University of Stirling has acquired some very interesting material from the Glassert estate at Aberfoyle. This is the first instalment, or so it is hoped, of what will be a much larger deposit of estate and family papers, and it certainly whets the appetite for what may follow. There is one personal diary for the year 1885, which rather stands in isolation, and five game books; two from the later nineteenth century (1874-1878, and 1885-1886,) and three from the second quarter of the twentieth century; 1925-1935, 1935-1939, and 1940-1942.

The diary for 1885, the author of whom is not given, but is clearly one of the senior members (perhaps on internal evidence Mary Hampson, whose husband then had the lease of the Glassert) sheds light on the everyday life of a well to do English family. Her life appears to have been a round of visiting and being visited, of letters sent and received (e.g. from Biarritz), of sermons heard and talks attended by themselves or friends. An entry for Saturday 21 March 1885 notes that one of the Joynsons (D[*orothy?*]) had called to report what a *"delightful meeting that they had hearing Miss Booth speak"*; perhaps the wife or daughter of the Salvation Army's General Booth? This family was part of what had become an established pattern of migration for quite a number of well-to-do English families, of going north to Scotland for the summer and the shooting. It had started fifty years or so earlier with parties of young men roughing it on the moors, but by this period, thanks to better transport and accommodation, the whole household – ladies, servants, children – was decamping north. And they were going earlier in the year: in the late spring or early summer, not just for the glorious twelfth, returning only in the autumn. This particular family departed their English home in mid May and set out for Scotland, as the diarist concisely records (Wed., 13 May 1885)

> *Left for Scotland. Altringham Station at 1 o'clock . Met Jane Forshar at Victoria Station Manchester. Left at 2.30 Arrived in Edinburgh at 8.40 – drove to the Royal, had an excellent dinner and a good night.* [Thursday] *Did a little shopping – called on Mr Patterson – went to the Academy and left for Aberfoyle in afternoon. Arrived at the Glassert about 7 o'clock.'*

It was a steady, unflustered, predictable railway journey: very different from fifty years earlier when the first outriders had forayed north by boat and coach. The family's link to the area had started in 1833, or so Peter Joynson has suggested in his compilation *Local Past*, when Edward Joynson and a friend toured the Trossachs, prompted by Scott's *Rob Roy*. Enchanted with Loch Ard, they resolved to return and did so some sixteen years later when in 1849 they leased shootings in the area from the Duke of Montrose. The bachelor gathering of young sportsmen using bothies, forming and reforming syndicates, was later to lead to colonisation by their extended family, building or renovating substantial properties for their summers. The Hampsons took Couligartan in 1852 and later Glassert (1865): the Jones Duchray Castle, and William Joynson (then 70) leasing Alstkeith house and the shootings at Ledard from Whitsun 1871. The 1874 gamebook starts with a summary of game killed, – "*our fifth year*".

The game books are not just bare records of what was shot, where and when, and by whom, but are thickened by comment, as to how the dogs worked, what the weather was like, who shot well, and which drives worked. Some of this is humdrum; – e.g. August 12 1876 "*a very hot day. Walter Barratt with Peter and two brown dogs shot the moor east of Tinkler but did not find birds plentiful*". But there are also notes of occurrences, a woodcock carrying her young, a grouse chased by a hawk into some railings. The later volumes contain letters to *The Field* on shooting matters, including long runs of bags, photographs and drawings. There are biographies of the keepers, perhaps prepared for retirement presentations, such as Peter McAlpine who retired in 1945 after thirty-three years' service. There are glimpses of family history: there is a note in the game book for 1942 that Captain Joynson, a major in the Black Watch home battalion, had died of wounds sustained accidentally in a Home Guard exercise on August 3, 1942. To a considerable extent, Peter Joynson has already quarried the game books in his *Local Past*, which was published in 1996 and is an eclectic and valuable volume of life in and around Aberfoyle. This draws on these game books and other family material for recollections and observation, as well as splicing in information from, for example, the Statistical Accounts. In his introduction, Mr Joynson acknowledged that much of the information had been extracted from his father's "comprehensive game books and other writings".

What is the value of this accession?

First it gives an insight into the sporting – golf as well grouse features large – and general interests of a landed family. Religion brooks large; committed Anglicans in England, they were as keen episcopalians in Scotland, and were active supporters of the church at Aberfoyle. They took a deep interest in the natural history of the area. Peter Joynson's father and uncle – Ralph – were keen and knowledgeable observers of the land, and in the game books took time to analyse the records of bags. He wanted to know why numbers of game and other species varied. A letter of his to the Field, '*Blackcock and Pheasants*', using his own estate records, was published in September 1924. His hypothesis was that the increase in pheasants was directly linked to the decrease in blackgame; his surmise was that the male blackcock was outfought by the cock pheasant with its spurs. Dogs were a particular passion of his and his brother Ralph. The first spaniels had been introduced on the estate two generations previously in 1872, and retrievers in 1876, whereas before only pointers or setters had been used for walking up. An entry for July 7 1934 records the death by sunstroke of Belt, aged about 8, "the last of our setters and pointers". The spaniels that the Joynsons bred, trained and worked, became renowned, and had considerable success in field trial championships. In February 1937, or so the game book records, one dog was sold for the very considerable sum of £120 to an American, Martin Hogan of Illinois. Sent out by the Queen Mary, it went on to be a field trials champion in the USA.

There is much, as might be expected on the management of the moors, on the techniques tried to preserve the grouse stock and then to harvest them once the season started. 6-8 brace of Yorkshire birds were put down at Dunruig in 1895, as part of an experiment to improve the local stock. Originally, as with all Highland moors, all the days involved walking up with dogs. Driving, by which the birds were brought by beaters to the guns in butts, was only introduced in early 1890s, (cf 'Notes on Game', "*Driving really started in 1896 though the first drive attempted actually took place in 1890*"). This technique allowed the less fit and the more elderly good sport, and the siting of the butts took considerable planning. Indeed there was clearly adjustment and innovation as heather cover altered, with new drives tried. In August 1934, the game book records that Tinkler and West Gashoile were driven to experimental positions near the Gangers' Pass, "to great success". There were difficulties with the loss of ground to forestry, and problems with bracken. The last game book is of value in shedding light on what happened during the second world war when the general assumption is that game shooting came to an end.

Environmental historians will be interested in the quantitative evidence as to the recorded bags of game, good years and bad, peacetime and war, and indeed fortunes of the fishings in the area for which long runs – over decades – are recorded. Joynson had privileged access to material – estate records and other material – of real value, some of which has since disappeared. At the end of the Game book for 1934 he quotes from an old source – a hotel register- for 1862 to 1868 which lists boats, rods and catches on Loch Ard. He also mentions an Aberfoyle fishing club and refers to a fishing hut built on the island by the Stirling Fishing club in 1839. There are extensive and lengthy records for the fishings on other waters – Loch Katrine and the Lake of Mentieth. And, of course there are local incidents that add colour to our knowledge of the area. In 1922 poachers dynamited the Blacklinn on the Duchray water, taking eight fish. Game keepers, and water bailiffs had their work cut out.

There are wider questions which these sources alone cannot answer. We can sense what the Joynsons and others like them enjoyed in their Scottish summers. What we would wish to explore is what the economics of their estates were; how far English money underwrote the Highland experience, first as tenants and then as proprietors. Their love of field sports cost them money, but how much? Little, after all, was to be recouped from the sale of game; indeed the 1874 game book starts with a list of those to whom grouse were given; the minister and the schoolmaster each one brace, the church precentor 2 hares, and the post boy two rabbits. For what light we have, we are grateful; to what there may be, we look forward.